Riddles
Requiring Resolution
...for Christians

CLAUDE O. MCCOY, M.D.

Copyright © 2013 by Claude O McCoy, M.D.

All rights reserved. No part of this book may be used, reproduced, stored in a retrieval system, or transmitted in any form whatsoever — including electronic, photocopy, recording — without prior written permission from the author, except in the case of brief quotations embodied in critical articles or reviews.

All scripture quotations, unless otherwise indicated, are taken from the *Holy Bible, King James Version. KJV.* Public Domain.

FIRST EDITION

ISBN: 978-1-939748-16-4

Library of Congress Control Number: 2013942594

Published by
NewBookPublishing.com, a division of Reliance Media, Inc.
515 Cooper Commerce Drive, Suite 140, Apopka, FL 32703
NewBookPublishing.com

Printed in the United States of America

Disclaimer: The views and opinions expressed in this book are solely those of the authors and other contributors. These views and opinions do not necessarily represent those of New Book Publishing and Reliance Media Inc.

NBP

Acknowledgements

I am very grateful to my friends Kay and Gary Bannister.

At a time of deep personal despair, they gave me a monograph that was instrumental in starting me on a journey of understanding the reality of the LIFE that God had given to me. As a consequence of that journey, my approach to counseling was revolutionized. I recognized that I needed to correct my own thinking before I could begin to be of any significant help to others.

I would also like to acknowledge the persons who provided invaluable assistance in reviewing and editing this manuscript. Thanks to Pastor Jim Shemaria, Dr. Larry Bailey, and my longtime friend Gary Bannister.

Paul's Relevant Prayer
Ephesians Chapter 1

[15] "Wherefore I also, after I heard of your faith in the Lord Jesus, and love unto all the saints,[16] Cease not to give thanks for you, making mention of you in my prayers;[17] That the God of our Lord Jesus Christ, the Father of glory, may give unto you the spirit of wisdom and revelation in the knowledge of him:[18] **The eyes of your understanding being enlightened**; that ye may know what is the hope of his calling, and what the riches of the glory of his inheritance in the saints,[19] And what *is* the exceeding greatness of his power to us-ward who believe, according to the working of his mighty power,[20] Which he wrought in Christ, when he raised him from the dead, and set *him* at his own right hand in the heavenly *places*,[21] Far above all principality, and power, and might, and dominion, and every name that is named, not only in this world, but also in that which is to come:"

Special Reading Instructions

English is sometimes a very imprecise language. The ancient Greek language was much more precise in a variety of ways. For example, they had several different words to differentiate among the various kinds of love. Much of this book is focused on the discussion and meaning of the word, life. It is a fundamental premise of this book that a great deal of confusion arises from the failure of Christians to recognize that there are different concepts of what life is. The author seeks to differentiate between the two forms of life described herein by the spelling of the word and the use of punctuation marks.

The eternal life that comes from God will be spelled "Life."

The normal usage of the word life will be spelled life.

Table of Contents

Acknowledgements 3

Prologue 11

Introduction 15

Chapter 1
    The Riddle of Romans 7: The Problem Portrayed .. 21

Chapter 2
    The Riddle of Romans 7: The Analysis 31

Chapter 3
    Changed Behavior 51

Chapter 4
    Changed Behavior (Continued) 67

Chapter 5
    The Gods Must Be….Are Crazy!?? 77

Chapter 6
    The Riddle of the Christians' Abundant "LIFE" 87

Chapter 7
    The Process of Laying Hold of "LIFE" 115

Chapter 8
    Tips From the Counseling Office 127

About the Author 133

Prologue

Proverbs 16:25 "There is a way that seemeth right unto a man, but the end thereof [are] the ways of death."

On planet Earth, all of God's children have troubles. Most of our biggest troubles come from acting and thinking normally about life! In other words, we have been acting in the way that seems right described in Proverbs 16:25. The critical issue is what to do with our troubles. If the troubles we experience are depriving us of the experience of "Life" and peace, then it should be a wakeup call that something is not right. God promises perfect peace to all His children who put their trust in Him.

If your journey has not brought you to a place of peace, then you need to be aware that you are trapped in a **riddle**

requiring resolution. The reason you are in this condition in most cases is ignorance of the reality that you are thinking about and processing life normally. In other words, you are operating in a way that *seems* right (Proverbs 16:25), but which leads to the experience of death and not "Life" and peace. You may be surprised to know that almost all people who seek professional counseling do so for a single reason. However, they have many ways of describing why they are seeking counseling.

The reason most adults seek professional counseling is they are convinced that some person or some circumstance has interfered with the creation of, or the acquisition of, or the apprehension of what they perceive their life for today to be. Conclusion: such people are delusional! A delusion is a false belief. In reality, no person, circumstance, or thing can prevent a Christian from experiencing "Life" and peace unless they allow this to happen either through ignorance or lies. Normal thinking people are convinced that life is a matter of degree. If only their troubles could go away or at least diminish, then they would have more life and come a bit closer to a place of peace. This also is a delusion.

Contrary to normal thinking, "Life" is not a matter of degree. "Life" is all or none. A person cannot be half-alive.

"Life" is like white light. If you take white light and pass it through a prism, you can see all the colors of the rainbow. So it is with "Life." "Life" is composed of a whole series of constituent elements that collectively make up "Life." If a person has "Life," he must have it all! It is a great mystery amongst evangelical Christendom that "Life" begins the instant you receive it.

Evangelicals are absolutely correct in their mission to warn all people that to secure "Life," hope, and a future, they must acknowledge and trust in the substitutionary death of Jesus Christ. Those who trust in Christ have been labeled newborn "babes in Christ," and they are rightly encouraged to join a local church where they can be fed the "milk" of the "Word," that they might continue to "grow in Christ." The feeding programs that most are subjected to have a heavy concentration of information as to how a Christian *should* act and be. They are often encouraged to try hard to live a good "Christian life." Initially, babies do need milk. In real life, babies who are not started on solid food in a timely manner and continue to receive only milk become overweight and sickly. There is a parallel spiritual truth. Christians who are fed a steady diet of milk also get sick.

God doesn't want you to try to live a good "Christian

life"! The reason is, you can't. God wants you to be a vessel through which Christ's "Life" can be expressed (walked out). The eternal "Life" that has been given to the believer is the very "Life" of God! It is his "Life" and power that ensures success. Failure is assured if you have been thinking about and processing your life "normally," i.e., "the way that seems right." It is a truism that no one can correct a problem until they can first identify the problem. If it seems that your success is being blocked by a riddle, please read on.

Introduction

"Blessed is the Christian who has
a clear and conscious awareness that his life
is beset with...
Riddles Requiring Resolution."

Claude McCoy, M.D.

There is a rather common pattern for spiritual development. For most of us, it begins with the hearing and reckoning to be true of what has been called "The Gospel of Good News for Sinners." We come to understand that we are hopeless sinners, cut off from God, the source of all "Life." We also learn of God's love for us expressed through his provision of reconciliation by faith in the sacrificial death of Christ. Armed and often excited with this new revelation of God's love for us and the hope of sometime enjoying heaven's delights, we want everyone to know of the new hope, joy, and freedom that we have found in our new relationship with Christ.

As the days pass, our knowledge of God continues to grow. It is enhanced through a variety of paths, which can include personal reading of scripture, church attendance, sharing with Christian friends, etc. Some of us are first introduced to riddles through the reading of scriptures. An intelligent person will quickly see that the Bible seems frequently to speak in riddles. For example, Paul stated in 2 Corinthians 12:10 that when he was weak was when he was strong, which is a riddle.

The scripture in Ephesians 4:15 instructs Christians to "speak the truth in love." to all and yet James 3:8 states, "the tongue can no man tame", another riddle.

Curiously, as our knowledge of God grows, in a parallel manner, for some, the glow of our initial excitement and joy begins slowly to wane. As we become increasingly caught up in our efforts to cope with the vicissitudes of day-to-day experience, our hope that we can free ourselves from our old, sinful lives begins to falter. We often are surprised to find ourselves drifting back into old patterns of thinking and behavior. Old habit patterns begin to re-emerge and to dominate our lives. The reality that we are not entirely in control of our personal universe begins to gnaw upon our consciousness. Life is not turning out as we had hoped. The things that we had been looking to for our satisfaction no longer satisfy us or bring the fulfillment for which we had been hoping. Some of these things instead have produced great pain and emptiness.

Many attempt to control the pain of this emerging awareness through some form of denial. We attempt to avoid, minimize, and project blame for our life dilemmas. The pain associated with the knowledge that our life is a riddle usually mounts until we can no longer deny it. The excitement and joy of our initial love affair with God seems to give way to painful experiences, perplexities, and disillusionments. As a consequence of our spiritual education, we know more and more about how we **should** live, but are unable to implement it. People around us may urge us to "try harder." We also come to know more and more about what we shouldn't do, but that is exactly what we continue to do.

To put it another way, we begin to see that our life does not approximate what the scripture sets forth as the hoped for "norm" for Christian experience. In other words, we are not experiencing "Abundant LIFE" and "Peace." As a consequence of these moments of pain, the stage is being set for the next phase of spiritual growth. To accomplish the task of this phase of growth successfully requires the resolution of certain common riddles. It is also at this time that many seek counseling. Regrettably, in many instances, counseling leads to further disillusionment, because the counseling does not address the universal set of spiritual riddles requiring resolution that underlie most counseling problems.

There is a set of three centrally important riddles that cause the greatest perplexity for most people. These riddles must be resolved in order to continue spiritual growth and development. It is the purpose of this book to provide the knowledge for the resolution of these three riddles. Knowledge alone, however, does not guarantee the successful resolution of the riddles. Knowledge is necessary for the basis of resolution; however, there are other required steps, which we will discuss.

In this book, we shall examine the following three critically important **Riddles Requiring Resolution:**
1. The Riddle of Romans 7:
   The person who knows what he should do and doesn't do it, and the person who does what he knows he shouldn't.

2. The Riddle of Personal Powerlessness:

   The central universal riddle imbedded in the first riddle

3. The Riddle of our "Abundant LIFE."

   The greatest mystery facing all Christians.

One or more of these three riddles in some manner underlie almost every counseling problem.

As we consider these **Riddles Requiring Resolution**, I hope you will examine yourself as to whether you have learned their centrally important message and lessons. In the next chapter, we will illustrate the problem of Romans 7, using fictional stories made up from real life experiences of others. All people have experienced Romans 7. How have *you* experienced or how are you currently experiencing it?

CHAPTER 1

The Riddle of Romans 7: The Problem Portrayed

For 50, years I have listened to the stories of real persons in pain. I heard stories from some who knew what they should do and could not bring themselves to do what they should. And I heard stories from others who knew what they shouldn't do and just couldn't stop. The following vignettes are fictional accounts similar to the real life stories.

Knowing What To Do and Not Doing It:
Jim and Joy:

Jim and Joy, both Christians, had been married for 22 years. The first years of their marriage were fun and exciting. They were preoccupied with getting Jim's business started, creating a home and starting a family. Initially, they were regular church attendees. In those days life was busy and full, and it seemed that they were working on common goals. As the years went by, Jim continued to spend a lot of time at his business. He also joined the local country club allegedly to have access to golfing, which was his favorite hobby. He told Joy that he needed this membership to entertain business customers.

For her part, Joy hoped that as Jim's business became established, he would be spending more time with her and the children. But the truth was that they were slowly drifting apart. Once all of the children were in school, Joy found herself with a lot of time on her hands. Because of Jim's continuing absences, Joy began to turn to other activities to fill her day. When Jim started entertaining his customers by golfing at the club on both Saturday and Sunday, Joy joined a nearby health club and started taking aerobics classes.

Whenever she tried to talk to Jim about spending more time with her, Joy was rebuffed and told that she was being unappreciative of all the efforts he was making to provide her and the children with the finer things in life. When she asked him about why he would never go to church with her, Jim said that although he felt badly about missing so much church, weekends were his customers' best times to get together with him.

As time went by, a new male aerobics instructor took over Joy's class and began to give her more and more attention. She was initially flattered by the attentions of a person willing to provide her with what Jim was unwilling to do. In no time at all, Joy was spending more and more time with the instructor and became certain she was in love with him. Soon, Joy confronted Jim, told him about her new love, and asked him for a divorce. Jim was shocked and insisted that Joy come with him to see their pastor.

At that meeting, the pastor confronted Jim with his failure to fulfill his responsibilities to the family. He asked Joy if she would be willing to give Jim another chance. She refused, and said that she had attempted to talk to him about his workaholism for years, and she was through trying. The pastor pointed out that she did not have a scriptural basis for a divorce, and Jim had indicated that he would work on spending more time with her. Joy knew that she should separate herself from her new paramour and give Jim a chance, but she just couldn't. She and Jim were divorced three months later.

Sally:

Sally had been raised in a very dysfunctional family. Her

father was an alcoholic who was physically and emotionally abusive to her throughout her childhood. Her mother was a weak person unable to protect Sally from her father's abuse. Sally married at the age of 18 just to get out of her family. After that, Sally cut herself off from all contact with her parents, but maintained contact with a younger sister.

At age 22, Sally came to know Christ. She still suffered from panic attacks that began when she was 10, and had never gone away. She sought counseling for these at a local Christian Counseling service. In the midst of counseling, she received word from her sister that her father, with whom she had not spoken in years, had been hospitalized with severe cirrhosis of the liver and was not expected to live. Her sister reported that he knew he was dying and wanted to make his peace with Sally before he went, so was asking to see her.

Sally discussed this request with her therapist, who talked with her about the importance of forgiving her father and its bearing on her own recovery from abuse. Sally stated that the therapist had no concept of what he was asking her to do. Although she knew the Bible often mentioned forgiveness, she simply could not bring herself either to visit or to forgive her father who had caused her and her entire family so much pain and terror from his drinking and abusive behavior. Sally believed the fact that he was about to die from the consequences of his drinking was his just deserts. As a result of their disagreement, Sally felt that she could not return to counseling.

Fred:

Fred was an only child who grew up on a farm. His parents were very non-communicative, withdrawn, and unsociable people who hardly spoke, even to each other. As a result, Fred grew up in an atmosphere of social and emotional isolation. There were no children his age living near the farm, so Fred had little social contact outside of school. Fred's father was busy all day with farming and when his chores were finally done, he came home and either watched television or read the newspaper until he went to bed. Fred's mother seemed only to cook and clean her house. The only thing the family did together was watch an occasional movie and attend church weekly.

After graduation, Fred met Phyllis at a church social. She had just moved to town. It was love at first sight. Phyllis was an exuberant and outgoing person. Fred admired her capacity to talk and relate, and was immediately attracted to her. She saw Fred as a strong, silent type who gave her no competition in conversation, at which she an expert. They were married shortly after they met, and several children soon came along. Although Phyllis was initially somewhat taken aback with Fred's aloofness, she passed it off as being of little consequence. He always seemed happy to see her when he came home from work, and was very consistent in his church attendance with her. She was sure that when they had children, it would seem more like they were a family.

However, as the children arrived and began to grow up, Phyllis noticed that she was continuing to do most of the parenting. Fred spent most of his time watching television and ignoring their children as they played around him. Phyllis talked with Fred on a number of occasions about taking more interest in the children and spending more time with them. Each time, he would promise to heed her request and give attention to the children, but would not follow through. Eventually, Fred confided to Phyllis that whenever he remembered he needed to spend time with the children, he had an indescribable feeling inside him. He said he didn't feel comfortable playing with the children and he just didn't know what to do or what to say to them.

Knowing What You Shouldn't Do and Doing It:
Terri:

Terry was a very social person who seemed to relate well to everyone. Her husband had been very successful in business and provided a beautiful home complete with a live-in maid who cooked and cleaned for Terri five days a week. It seemed that all was well in Terri's life. But her apparent social confidence was a cover for a deep unfulfilled need to feel accepted. In her younger years, she had learned that she could acquire a sense of acceptance by providing her friends with tidbits of gossip, for which she was always on the lookout. She came to believe, "Have you heard about ...." was her ticket to being accepted by her peers. And there always seemed to be willing ears for the tidbits of gossip she constantly mined from every social contact.

Becoming a Christian and joining the local church did not change her way of relating. In fact, just the opposite occurred. Terri saw her church as a fantastic new pond in which to fish in order to fill her desperate need to find acceptance. Initially, it seemed that all was going well with hew new church acquaintances, and most of the women welcomed her warmly. But as Terri repeated her efforts to find the acceptance she desired by gossiping, the women of the church slowly seemed less and less inclined to welcome her into their social activities. Terri noticed this, and she also felt certain that the pastor's sermon on gossiping was aimed directly at her.

She decided to stop gossiping, but found she could not stop. One day, a mature woman from the church called and asked to meet with her. After feeling somewhat shunned for a while, Terri was delighted that someone was again showing her some attention. But the meeting was a disaster for her. When the woman lovingly explained the other women were avoiding her because of her gossiping, Terri felt so badly that she left the church. Shortly thereafter, she joined a new congregation and immediately began gossiping with the women who attended. The pattern was repeating itself.

Jack:

Jack had grown up in an average middle-class family that made an effort to teach him values. He had found Christ as a teen and become involved in the local church youth group. As he grew older, Jack had a regular job but had also developed a part-time business that he operated on a strictly cash basis. The January following his first year of marriage, his new wife questioned not finding any entries of

Jacks sideline business on the Internal Revenue Report forms. He told her he wasn't making all that much money from his sideline business and just didn't feel that he needed to take all the time to make out all the extra forms required for the second business. This became an annual point of contention whenever he asked his wife to sign the IRS form with missing information regarding his additional income.

Sandra:

Sandra began smoking as a teen when a girlfriend offered her a cigarette. Soon, she began meeting with her friend and other teen smokers just off the school property to have a smoke and talk before school and during lunch hour. School authorities would not punish them as long as they were off school property. She thought smoking was cool, and all the kids in the smoke group accepted her. She smoked 2 packs a day for the next 20 years. And, as the years went by, she found that a smoke could help her relax and feel less tense. She believed that the warning on the packages applied to other people, that she was healthy and always would be.

After a while, she developed a little cough, but told herself, "All smokers cough a little. Mine isn't all *that* bad." Then one day, she coughed up blood. Her doctor diagnosed an early stage lung cancer and recommended she stop smoking immediately. She had lung surgery, which was a success. Afterward, her doctor urged her not to smoke. She agreed. But on her first trip shopping after the surgery, she passed the cigarette counter and wondered what it would be like to have just one smoke. After telling herself one wouldn't be all that bad, she bought a pack. Of course, others followed that one smoke and in no time at all she was smoking regularly again.

This problem of knowing what to do and not doing it and/or knowing what you shouldn't do and doing it are experiences universal to all. These vignettes you have just read are fictional examples of this common human experience. For those people who seek to live a God-honoring life, such circumstances represent **Riddles Requiring Resolution**. In the next chapter, we will examine the riddle's origins and its significance in the human experience.

Before reading on, why not stop and reflect on you own life? Are there things that you know you should be doing but you can't bring yourself to do? Are there things that you know you shouldn't be doing, but you just can't seem to stop? If you have identified such dilemmas in your life, this book is for you.

CHAPTER TWO

The Riddle of Romans 7: The Analysis

Romans 7:22 For I delight in the law of God after the inward man:
Romans 7:18b ...for to will is present with me; but how to perform that which is good I find not.
Romans 7:19 For the good that I would I do not: but the evil which I would not, that I do.
Romans 7:24 O wretched man that I am! who shall deliver me from the body of this death?

These verses show one of the foremost universal dilemmas of the human experience. We first experienced this painful perplexity in our youth. In subsequent years, we confronted it over and over again, but not always consciously. Most of us have great personal familiarity with this quandary long before we read about it in the Bible. The pains of increasing life experiences tend to sharpen our focus and awareness of this riddle's existence. The implications and consequences of our decisions and behaviors mount and lead to larger and larger internal anguish and pain. The larger the anguish of life a person experiences, the greater his or her capacity to identify with the lament of verse 24.

Counseling offices are filled with people trapped in the throes of the Romans 7 riddle with its attendant suffering. Many people seeking counseling already know the course they should take. But some cannot find it in themselves to follow the godly path, and others consciously do not wish to follow the path because to do so would, in their perception, cause more unbearable pain. Conversely, others are on ungodly paths they know they should abandon. However, they either cannot find it in themselves to step off the path or they perceive that doing so would cause more unbearable pain.

Let us begin our analysis of the Riddle of Romans 7 by looking at the positive qualities of the narrative. The speaker seems to be a sincere person who loves God and wants to do the right thing. In other words, he wants to be walking on a godly path. In order to delight in the law of God, we must assume that the person has a measure of knowledge of both God and His law. The speaker also possesses both the faculty of will power and the desire to do right. Alas, in spite of all these positive qualities, (sincerity, knowledge, willpower, and good intent) the speaker simply can't live in a God-honoring manner. Verse 24 is the consummate lament of a person who is squarely facing this critically important **Riddle Requiring Resolution,** "O wretched man that I am! Who shall deliver me from the body of this death?"

If we examine the Romans 7 passage further, we would find three significant elements the speaker is missing:

1. A "way" to be successful is missing.
2. The person is hopeless and functioning in bondage (lacks freedom).
3. The person is experiencing "death," not "LIFE and Peace."

The resolution of the Romans 7 riddle would require access and possession of these three missing ingredients. It is the purpose of this book to acquaint the Christian reader with these necessary elements for success.

Where did all this trouble begin? When did the riddle of Romans 7 emerge? The answer is the Garden of Eden. The rebellion of Adam and Eve had catastrophic implications for the entire human race that would follow. Adam and Eve were gravely altered as a consequence of their rebellion, and the changes that occurred to them are passed along genetically to the whole human race. It is essential to have a clear understanding of the ways in which what happened in Eden affects everyone born afterwards. Let us examine what happened in Eden and its implications for the riddle of Romans 7.

The Consequences of Eden's rebellion:
1. Lost "LIFE"
2. Universal Bondage
3. Changed Thinking
4. Changed Emotions
5. Changed Behavior (Lost Way)

1. Lost "LIFE":

1 Corinthians 15:22   For as in Adam all die, even so in Christ shall all be made alive.

Disobedience severed Adam and Eve from their "Life" source (God). As a consequence of their actions, all of their offspring were born dead. When you were born, you also were born dead. I have a dangling vine in my office that has suffered greatly to demonstrate this point to my counselees.

When needing to illustrate how life is lost, I have frequently reached up and pulled a leaf from the vine, held it before my client, and asked," Is the leaf before you alive or dead?"

It is true that the chemistry within the individual cells of the leaf continues to function for a period following the leaf's being severed from the life source and, in a sense, the leaf appears to be alive for a time. However, the instant the leaf was severed from its life source, it died. Forces were set in motion at that instant which make it absolutely certain that unless the leaf is reconnected to a life source, it will most assuredly die. Because of Adam and Eve's disobedience, they were disconnected from the "Life" source and consequently lost their "Life." You, however, have already been reconnected to the "Life" source through your faith in Jesus Christ, although being reconnected to the "Life" source does not automatically lead to the experience of abundant "Life." The lack of the experience of the "Abundant Life" is an element contributing to the riddle of Romans 7.

If I were to leave the severed leaf on my desk for a week, it would begin to look like it is dead, which it would be. It takes people 70 years, more or less, to look the way they are when they arrive here, which is also dead. Christians have been reconnected to the "Life" source. However, that does not mean they automatically walk in "Life." It only means that "Life" is there for them.

2. Universal Bondage:

Hebrews 2:15 And deliver them who through fear of death were all their lifetime subject to bondage.

Bondage is another of three elements creating the Romans 7 riddle. Disobedience plummeted the whole human race into bondage to what the Bible defines as the fear of death. The manner in which this bondage manifests itself primarily and secondarily will be discussed in the subsequent section designated: Changed Behavior. The fear of death relates to the fear of not acquiring "Life." The person who is bound is entrapped in an endless stream of lies. The most significant and incredible lie will be discussed in the next section.

Most of us do not spend a lot of time contemplating the implications of this universal bondage upon our lives. In fact, since the bondage is universal, most of us don't even have a conscious awareness of its existence. It would be a wise endeavor to be aware of its existence and its daily effects upon our lives so we can take corrective action. Many Christians seem to believe that trusting Christ has automatically led to freedom from the genetic legacy of Eden's disobedience. Indeed, they have been judicially and positionally been set free. Functionally, however, they are still bound by the riddle of Romans until they appropriate their freedom.

3. Changed Thinking

Proverbs 16:25 There is a way that seemeth right unto a man, but the end thereof are the ways of death.

As a result of their disobedience Adam and Eve's thinking processes were dramatically changed. They began to think in a way that seems right to man, that leads to death. The scripture calls this kind of thinking "carnal" or "natural" thinking." Let me give you some examples of how their thinking was changed.

There are Degrees of "LIFE":

People began to believe that there are degrees of "Life." Join me anywhere people congregate and together, we could select people at random and ask them, "How much life do you have?" Most people would respond to us as if to add up the columns regarding their current life circumstances. It seems obvious to most that the happily married, healthy millionaire has more life than the recently unemployed person who is separated from their spouse and has health problems.

All "normal thinking" persons function as if there are degrees of life. People tend to look at the status of their family, their material possessions, their career status, etc. as an indication of how much life they have. According to a normal worldview, how much life you have is directly related to your circumstances. As a consequence of their thinking, circumstantial losses are equated to a loss of life. Circumstances begin to control how a person is experiencing life and how they feel.

Reality:

"Life" is all or none! Life is composed of a whole series of constituent elements which, when taken together, make up "Life." So if a person has "Life," they must have all the constituent elements that make up "Life." A person cannot be half-alive!

Life is a Do-It-Yourself Project:

Another expression of this faulty thinking is the idea that "Life" is a "do it yourself" project. It is something you are supposed to do yourself. You are supposed to go out and create your own life through your personal accomplishments and your efforts at finding things that meet your needs. If you are a Christian, you should also try to live a good "Christian life" in the process of attempting to create your own life. The way you do that is through marriage or career, children, family, health, friends, etc. Others join one group or another group, or do this and do that with the underlying motive to get their own needs met as opposed to serving others. "Do it yourself!" is the normal worldview. This is how people think they need to go about creating, acquiring, or apprehending life.

The church and all of society are all offspring of Adam and Eve. They are genetically dosed or "hardwired" with this kind of thinking by virtue of being born. Becoming a Christian does not automatically mean that one's thinking is automatically corrected.

Reality:

Human beings are not gods. No one can create any "Life" at all! What a normal thinking person believes life is has nothing to do with "Life." These things in actuality are supposed to be blessings in addition to "Life." (We shall discuss this further in the next chapter.)

4. Changed Emotions:

When Adam and Eve became disobedient, they began to experience a whole host of new emotions that they had not previously experienced. Most of these new emotions do not tell the truth. In order for us to talk about emotions, I would like to pause and give a definition of "emotion." We could offer a dictionary definition; however, I consider those definitions somewhat lacking. Consequently, I have made up my own definition:

"Emotions are life qualifiers that make non-cognitive, non-volitional characterizing statements about our life."

They are non-cognitive, in the sense that they are not directly connected to thinking. For example, suppose I said to you, "Would you please become angry?" Would you begin to feel angry? Probably not. But if I and slapped you in the face and then asked you to become angry, you would more than likely experience the feeling. This is because emotions are indirectly connected to thinking. In other words, thinking needs to be connected in some way to a context before you begin to feel emotion. Emotions are non-volitional, in the sense that they cannot be controlled. No one can control his or her emotions. Even God incarnate, in the Garden of Gethsemane, did not control his emotions. You cannot simply turn emotions off. You cannot make them go away with willpower. The task of dealing with emotions is not to try to control them, but rather to process them in a way that honors God so that they don't have to take us hostage and bring us into bondage.

The last thing in the definition of emotions is that they make characterizing statements about our life. And so to understand "Life," we need to also define "Life." The word and its antithetical opposite, death, are familiar to us. We generally use them when we are talking about the life or death of the body. That is not what I am referring to now, however. Christians sometimes use the words life and death when they talk about a future "Life" or future death. But that is not what I am referring to, either. What we are talking about is the "Life" or death that we experience in the here and now. Examples of "Life" in the here and now would be to have good self-esteem and a sense of significance, to be acceptable, to be complete, to be secure, and to have hope. Death in the here and now would be the opposite. This means to have poor self-esteem and feelings of insignificance, and to feel unacceptable, insecure, hopeless, and so on. Our emotions make characterizing statements about our life.

When Adam and Eve were disobedient and turned away from God to pursue their life apart from Him, they began to experience emotions they had not previously experienced. I would like to review their situation before they were disobedient, and then review their situation after they were disobedient.

Before they were disobedient, Adam and Eve looked to God as their "Life" source. The Old Testament is filled with the statement, "Fear the Lord." The root motivating force of Adam and Eve's life was their fear or awe of God as the creator, provider, and sustainer of their lives. This root motivating force was differentiated in accordance with the three parts of their intangible personalities. The Bible says that everybody has a heart, a mind, and a conscience. And so, in their **mind**, Adam and Eve had the capacity to experience the anger that God has, which is described as righteous anger. There is an Old Testament verse that says, *"The fear of the LORD is to hate evil."* In their **heart**, they had the capacity, to experience strong confidence. *Proverbs 14:26 "In the fear of the LORD is strong confidence."* And because they had not yet disobeyed God, they had a pure **conscience**, and their conscience affirmed them.

When they became disobedient, they began to experience emotions that were mirror images of what they had experienced previously. Their fear of God was exchanged for the **"fear of death."** The "fear of death" became Adam and Eve's new root motivating force. The scripture in Hebrews (2:15) says that Christ came to free those, who though their fear of death were subject to bondage throughout their lives. The bondage that is described in Romans 7 originated in the Garden of Eden, in the rebellion of Adam and Eve. Because we are Christians does not mean that we automatically function freely. We have been judicially set free from that bondage; but unless we appropriate that freedom, we continue to be bound up with the same bondage of Adam and Eve.

This new root motivating force (the "fear of death"), was also differentiated in a mirror image fashion to what was the case previously. For example, I said in their hearts, Adam and Eve had the capacity to experience strong confidence. What is the opposite of strong confidence? It is anxiety. Anxiety comes out of the heart and says, "I'm afraid that I am not going to have a life." Anxiety has many cousins: nervousness, chronic anxiety, panic attacks, hyperventilation syndrome, agoraphobia, etc. All of anxiety's cousins say the same thing as anxiety, which is, "I am afraid that I am not going to have a life."

The opposite of Godly anger is human anger, and so the scripture says the wrath of man does not fulfill the righteousness of God, because the wrath of man fulfills man's righteousness. Human anger comes out of the mind and its main messages are, "Somebody or something is depriving me of my life and I'm mad about it," and "I am being victimized."

The manner of expression of our emotions was shaped by our early experiences, as our parents and significant others modeled the way to express emotions. Those who grew up in an emotional climate in which it was considered either not nice or dangerous to express anger openly will likely experience depression more than overt, conscious anger. Depression can represent a combination of things, and some folks are genetically more susceptible to depression. All of our emotions are mediated through chemistry. Some of us are genetically more sensitive to the mediation of internalized anger. I call it a "genetic amplifier." Emotionally generated depression occurs when human anger is internalized. This usually occurs after years of conditioning process.

I have seen many clients come in and say they are depressed. I often ask them, "Is there a possibility that you are angry?" Often, their history of not having told themselves the truth about their anger is so incredibly long and forceful that they are not even aware they are angry. They are just depressed. Something is wrong, and they do not know what or why. Others may say they are *not* angry, because they are not putting their fist through a wall or throwing things.

Depression is another one of the variations of emotionally generated human anger. There is also a depression that people can experience because something is physically wrong with their body. That is not what I am talking about; physiologically generated depression is not an expression of internalized anger.

The third change of emotion for Adam and Eve was in their conscience, as they began to experience guilt and shame. They began to have a conscience that condemned them, that began to say to them something like, "You are a failure, you don't measure up, and you are so terrible you don't even deserve a life."

In summary, there was a tremendous change in how Adam and Eve experienced their emotions. As a consequence of their disobedience, they began to experience new emotions that made negative qualifying statements about their lives. Many of these negative qualifying emotional statements do not tell the truth. In fact, almost every negative emotion that a Christian experiences does not tell the truth.

The Truth About Anxiety:

For a Christian the message of anxiety is a lie. Christian people already have "Life." It is possible for a Christian person not to experience abundant "Life," but it is not possible for a Christian person not to have "Life." And so human anxiety experienced by a Christian is a lie.

The Truth About Human Anger:

Human anger is a kind of anger that is qualitatively different than God's anger, because human anger says that somebody or something is depriving me of my life and I am mad about it. Human anger is telling me that I am being innocently victimized by others who are depriving me of my life. The scripture states that for those who have "Life," their life is hidden with Christ in God. So for a Christian human, anger is a lie

Colossians 3: 3 For ye are dead,
and your life is hid with Christ in God.

God himself is the defender of the Christian's "Life." Therefore, in reality, there is no event, person, or circumstance here that can deprive anybody of any "Life" at all. Of course, people on this planet can be very ugly. They can do dastardly deeds. They can be very mean; they can even go around and kill "earth suits." But there is one crime that cannot be committed by anybody on this planet: that is to deprive anybody here of any "Life" at all. It is impossible for anything that occurs on this planet to deprive anyone of any life at all! Human anger always lies. People can certainly hurt us badly, but they cannot deprive us of our "Life."

This knowledge can assist us in processing our anger and put it into perspective. It can help us not to sin in response to our anger. Most folks are not aware that their human anger is making a qualitative statement to them about their life. In most instances, it is telling them something is going on that in reality cannot be going on. Human anger attempts to establish our own righteousness. For example, let us pretend that you are my spouse. I am operating under the kind of thinking that I described earlier, that I have to create my own life, and the reason I married you was to get some life from you.

Since there is no way you can give me this life, somewhere along the line, I am probably going to get angry with you. And my anger is going to tell me that you are depriving me of my life and I am mad about it. And the beauty of that is that I do not have to look in the mirror and see a crazy man. If I am looking to you for part of my life, then I am not looking to God, the only source of "Life." Because of my anger, I don't have to look in the mirror and see the reality of what is going on within me. My anger is telling me that the problem is not in me, the problem is you. And so it is establishing my righteousness. It is telling me that you are innocently victimizing me and I am feeling as if you are depriving me of part of my life. This cannot be happening! Human anger always lies.

The Truth About Guilt and Shame:

Guilt and shame are perceived by a carnal mind as saying something like, "You are so terrible that you do not even deserve a life." The scriptures state that when a person becomes a Christian, according to 2 Corinthians 5:17, that God the Father makes that person a new creation. God causes that person to measure up, because He gives them intrinsic worth. He makes them beautiful. He makes all his children visions of loveliness. (However, His children may not always act like visions of loveliness.)

The purpose of guilt and shame is to cause us to deal with the issues in our life which are God-dishonoring. The problem is that most of us, when we respond to either guilt or shame, do so in a way that is God-dishonoring, which is to get into a self-punishment program or a self-improvement program, both of which dishonor God. Self-punishment dishonors God, because Christ has already suffered for our sins. What the father is looking for is a transformed life. Self-improvement is not possible, because we cannot change ourselves. For those who have received Christ and have been made new creations, God accomplished the necessary changes that we needed at the moment of faith. All the necessary changes that the Christian needs were accomplished when the Father made us new creations. He is waiting for us to appropriate those changes and to walk around in them.

Later in this book, we shall attempt to make the case that almost every negative emotion that a Christian experiences doesn't tell the truth. If you don't know what the truth is, what your emotions are saying is your truth. You become enslaved to your own lying emotions. In Chapter 3, I will discuss the way Adam and Eve's behavior was changed as a result of the fall. Their God-dishonoring behaviors flowed from their bondage, faulty thinking, and lying emotions.

Chapter Three

Changed Behavior

Power: The Primary Bondage

Adam and Eve's behavior was also changed as an expression of the bondage they fell into. The bondage is experienced on two levels, which can be described as primary and secondary bondage.

THE PRIMARY BONDAGE IS TO POWER.

The primary bondage to power is expressed in a way that is not obvious to the general population, yet all are caught up with it. The scriptures state, "The love of money is the root of all evil." Money is not the problem. It is what money represents, which is power. Adam and Eve turned away from God and began to pursue their life apart from God. I call this process of life pursuit apart from God the "power dance" for life. Life pursuing is based on an assumed philosophy that you must have some power to be able to create or acquire your life. Powerlessness is the worst thing that can happen to you if you are in life pursuit. If you are powerless, that means that you cannot "cut the mustard." If you can't "cut the mustard," that means you cannot create or acquire life. If you cannot create or acquire life, it is perceived as the worst possible disaster. People who are in life pursuit, whether they are aware of it or not, tend to express their bondage in the way they attempt to handle power.

REALITY ABOUT THE PRIMARY BONDAGE TO POWER:

No one has the power to create any "Life" at all!

Life pursuing is the pursuit of illusion. The two differing power styles of life pursuit apart from God also had their genesis in the Eden rebellion. The Genesis story began with God making man in His own image and in His own likeness. God brought the animals to Adam and Adam named the animals. And then God made an observation: within the animal kingdom, there was no fellowshipper for the man. So in that sense, Adam was not yet like God. So God put Adam to sleep, took a piece of his side, made another person, and then commanded this pair, Adam and Eve, to rule the world in which they found themselves. They were to do this ruling in a condition of complete and total equality, both brains working, and relating together in a fashion in which they did not violate each other's integrity. Satan then came along and seduced Eve with the idea that she could be the same as God. Satan implied that God's character was faulty in that He had withheld from them an essential quality of "Life." God had not done that, however. What He had withheld from them was the experiential knowledge of evil.

Eve was deceived and Adam joined her. As a result of their disobedience, they became carnal, fleshly beings. In Romans 8, Paul states that the carnal mind cannot be subject to God. God had commanded them to relate together in equality. Being unable to be subject to God because of their carnal mind meant equality was out and inequality was in. A carnal mind reasons that, if you and I are competitors for life and we are equal, I have no edge over you to make certain that if there is a limited amount of life resources available, I can be sure of acquiring what I need first. That is why life pursuers who feel their capacity to acquire life is threatened are likely to resort to inequality

There are two ways to be unequal to another person. One way is to operate in a position of power and superiority over another. The other condition of inequality is to function in a position of weakness and inferiority in relation to another person. There is a wide variety of behaviors that characterize a person who operates in power and superiority and, similarly, there is a variety of behaviors that characterize a person who operates in weakness and inferiority in relation to another person. There appear to be advantages to functioning from either position of power.

The Two Variables that Shape the Power Dance for Life:
1. Parental Model
2. Birth Order

There are two major variables that shape the way we normally handle power when we grow up and function as an adult. The first is the parental modeling found in the family that you are born into. In other words, it is how the mother and father in the home handle power. Parental modeling is the major variable that shapes the way people handle power. When I am working with people in a counseling situation, I very frequently ask them questions such as, "In your family of origin, who do you think wore the pants in the family?" or "In your family of origin, who made the most important decisions?" or "In your family of origin, how were conflicts resolved?" I ask these questions to get some sense of how their mom and dad handled the issues of power in their relationship. Were mom and dad grasping for power themselves, or reacting negatively against it?

Generally speaking, little boys want to be like their dads, and little girls like their mothers. So they usually identify with the style of the same sex-parent. There is one variation on that theme, however. In psychology, we call it a "reaction formation." A reaction formation is a psychological flip-flop. For example, if a little girl is raised in a family where her father is functioning from a position of strong power and has been overbearing and abusive to her mother, she may say to herself, "When I grow up I am never going to let a man do to me what my dad is doing to my mother." She will identify with her aggressor father's power style. When she grows up, she may be attracted to a man who functions as a wimp and begin beating up on him as her dad did to her mom. This is because she decided not to be a victim the way her mother was; she was going to be the aggressor.

Birth order is the second major variable that determines how people power dance when they grow up. Older children are used to taking charge of younger children, and making decisions for them. They are actually trained to do that in most families. The oldest children are more likely to act from positions of strong power. Youngest children, on the other hand are used to having things done for them, being told what to do, etc. Often, they adopt a weak power style. Only children never have anybody to fight with, so they frequently act the same as a person from a strong power position. This is because they have always had their way and never had anybody to challenge them.

With birth order, six years is a generation; so if six years occur between the birth of children, the birth order rules for power apply all over again to the younger siblings. Often, if you know two things about a person, you can usually predict the kind of overt conflicts they are going to complain about when they come to the counseling office. If you are a family counselor, you do not have to be too bright. You need to know only two facts. The first is, "How did Mom and Dad power dance together?" And the second is what is the birth order of each child. Knowing these two facts, you can usually predict the kinds of problems that people are going to tell you about.

When those two variables do not seem to be able to predict an accurate fit, there is often a reason. For example, if the oldest child was sickly, the second oldest may have functioned as the titular oldest and actually acted as the oldest. Some families are girl-focused and some families are boy-focused. In these cases, the boy or the girl gets special attention, which may skew the predictability of birth order as to as its influence on the way we manifest power.

Apparent Advantages to "Power Dancing" Styles

Let us now address the kind of behaviors that characterize strong power style and weak power style, and the apparent (but not real) advantages of each style.

Strong Power Style:

If you are operating in strong power style, you get to make the decisions, you get to act like your brain works, and you get your way. It is easy to see that if you are operating from a strong power style, it appears as if you are more likely to be able to get your needs met. People who operate from positions of strong power style say things like, "I do not care how you feel about it. You are going to do it my way." Or they may raise their voices and try to scare you into submission. The ultimate power maneuver is murder. The murderer feels like somebody is threatening his life. Consequently, he may reason that he must do away with this threat and regain control by getting rid of his tormenter. These are some of the advantages and behaviors which characterize functioning in strong power.

Weak Power Style:

People who operate from a position of weak power style generally have to depend upon the charity of others. The problem is, in the insane asylum called "Earth" there is not a whole lot of charity for people who operate from weak power style. Examples of a weak power style would be: 1. A "pathetic case." 2. A "dingy" person. 3. A doormat. 4. A "very nice" (life pursuing) person. The person who operates in weak power style is quite often a very, very nice person. That is one of the most common expressions of it. They are super nice and do nice things for everybody. When those who are very close to them do not respond to their niceness in the manner hoped for, they feel wounded and become angry. Often, because they are so nice, they internalize their anger and experience it as depression. This is a very common scenario for a person functioning in a weak power style.

The way the "nice" life pursuer thinks is as follows: "If I am willing to treat you very, very, very, nice, perhaps you will have compassion on me and meet my needs." Or, put another way, "I will love you, provided you will love me back." People who operate from weak power style generally are hoping that if they do their part, other people will respond and take care of them and meet their needs. (Only God can meet our need, which is the need for "Life"!)

Let me mention some advantages of the weak power style. One is to collect anger. People often do not respond to the nice person as the nice person wishes they would, which eventually makes the nice person angry. A wounded person can justify distance in a relationship if he or she is angry, which is one of the advantages to the weak power style. Distance provides safety from further hurt and wounding. The wounder cannot get close enough to control them if they are being kept at a distance by anger.

If you look into the heart of a person who makes a practice of weak power style, you usually will find a very angry person. These people collect and use their anger to maintain emotional distance in relationships with people who are operating from strong power. Another major advantage of the person functioning in weak power is that, if something goes wrong in the relationship, it always the other person who is at fault. The other person was operating in strong power style; they were the one who was operating as if their brain works and making decisions. Since the other person made the decisions, if something is wrong, it is obviously that person's fault. Weak power styles often procrastinate, and the ultimate weak power style maneuver is suicide.

Various Combinations of Strong and Weak Power Styles:

It follows, then, that there is a wide variety of possible combinations of power styles in relationships. For example, in some relationships, the man always acts in a strong power style, and the woman in the weak. In fact, some people say that is the way a Christian marriage is supposed to be, because the Bible seems to say that a man is supposed to be leader of the house, and the woman is supposed to be submissive. Actually, there is no combination of these kinds of power styles that is God honoring! No combination of power styles represents a Christian marriage. Remember that the basis of power dancing is rooted in a delusional system of being able to create one's own life.

In some marriages, the woman operates in the strong power style and the man operates in the weak power style. Other folks do psychological "flip-flops" which, as I stated earlier, the psychological professions call "reaction formations." Reaction formations (psychological flip-flops) can occur over years, or they can occur as quickly as you blink your eye. Take for example the woman who has functioned outwardly as a submissive wife, who has been doing it for years, and developing anger at her overbearing, strong power-style husband. Her husband has a great thing going. He has been having his way, and she has been getting angry, although remaining silent about it. Then, after years, she says, "I have had it. From now on you are going to do it my way." The wife exercises a reaction formation. She begins to act from a strong power style, and her husband thinks that she has gone crazy. He has two normal choices. One would be that he can stay the way he has been functioning, in which case, conflict is going to break out continuously, or, he can "flip-flop" and adopt a weak power style and enter into the illusion of some peace at home. There are other alternatives, but those are the two that are available to normal people.

There is a tendency for outsiders to feel sorry for such a wife. In reality, however, such a wife has been a mutual conspirator to this process. She and her husband share common insanity with power. The wife was being abused by her husband's strong power style; so in that sense, we can feel sympathy for her. However, she has been a conspirator with her husband in this process. She has initially enabled her husband's insanity and then switched to adopt her husband's carnal, strong power style, which is described in the cliché, "If you can't beat them, join them."

Regrettably, the Christian culture sometimes teaches women that they should adopt weak power styles. Again, no power dancing style is God honoring. Sometimes, two people with strong power styles marry. When they come for counseling, their complaint is, "We fight all the time." Sometimes, people with weak power styles marry. This is a conversation between weak power styles:

"Do you want to go out to supper tonight?"

"Oh I don't know. Do you want to go out?"

"It doesn't make any difference to me."

"Doesn't make any difference to me, either."

"Why don't you decide?"

"No. You decide!"

"Okay. Let's go out."

"Where do you want to go?"

"Oh, I don't know. Where do you want to go?"

"It doesn't make any difference to me."

"It doesn't make any difference to me either. Why

don't you decide?"

"..........................etc., etc."

This is a conversation between two people with working brains, acting like their brains are non-functional.

All combinations of power styles are God dishonoring. God has not changed his mind about marriage. Marriage is supposed to constitute a relationship between two whole people with both brains working. Married people are to relate together in a fashion that they do not violate each other's integrity, functioning together equally. To fulfill God's mandate for a God-honoring relationship of mutual equality requires a miracle for both the husband and the wife to accomplish. I will discuss this required miracle in a subsequent chapter.

We have been focusing on the marriage relationship; however, the same principals apply to other relationships that are God honoring. Healthy relationships only occur between two people who are relating together as equals and have both their brains functional.

Let's review the changed behavior caused by the distorted mental state that Adam and Eve experienced at the moment of their disobedience. You will recall that Adam and Eve turned away from God as their "Life" source and began to pursue their life apart from God. Life pursuit apart from God is based on an assumed philosophy that you have got to have some power to create your life. This problem of trying to create or acquire life runs into the problem of reality.

The Reality of the Power Dance:

No human being on this planet can create any "Life" at all. To function as though you can create your own life is to act as if you are a God. The creation of "Life" is the business of God. Men and women are not Gods. In his kindness and infinite patience, God permits reality to begin to crush us. We begin to feel frustrated in marriage, career, and the other places we are looking for life in the way that seems right. We begin to feel powerless. This is the most painful feeling that a normal person can experience. If you are powerless, it means you cannot create your life. Normal thinking believes that is the worst thing that can happen to you.

Normal Reactions to Early Encounters with Conscious Powerlessness:

There is a wide variety of things that Christians do to respond to early conscious feelings of powerlessness. Some begin to get anxious and worry over it. Our worry is telling us that we are afraid we are not going to have a life. If we are Christian, we already have our "Life." We are being deceived by a lying emotion. If we are in life pursuit, we are functioning as if we are totally unaware that we already have "Life." We believe our worry, a lying emotion that is saying to us that we are in jeopardy of not being able to acquire our life.

Some persons get angry. Their anger tells them that people or circumstances have been depriving them of life. Of course, the Bible says this cannot happen because the Christian's "Life" is hidden with Christ in God. People can do very hurtful things to each other. However, on Planet Earth, no one can deprive anyone else of any "Life" at all! Other folks look for their life in a career, and they do not find it. Their answer is to change careers. They go to another career and hope to find their life in that career. If they are not finding life with one spouse, they may get rid of that spouse and turn to another and look for life in him or her.

If all of this happens in mid-life, we call it a mid-life crisis. You have heard of someone who has been a family man and a good citizen, and worked at his job for 30 years; who suddenly resigns, buys a Harley-Davidson, divorces his wife, and buys a set of black leather and chains and runs away with a 14-year-old girl. We call that a mid-life crisis. This represents a massive turning away from where "Life" isn't to pursue life in another place where "Life" isn't. Of course, this sort of thing does not work. Reality keeps chasing us. We become frustrated and agonized in our life pursuits. Usually, this attitude begins to catch up with us when we are about 40 to 55 years of age. For those on a fast track, the frustration and pain can begin earlier. It takes many, but not all people a matter of time to learn that they have not found "Life" in all those places. Some Christians go to their grave in this state of anger and anxiety, and never realize that God has already given them "Life" for today.

When we attempt to create our own life, it leads to a sense of powerlessness, which may or may not be identified in our conscious awareness. Regardless of whether it is accurately identified in our consciousness, it is experienced as being incredibly painful. Some folks make a final effort to control the pain of life pursuit. We will discuss this next.

CHAPTER 4

Changed Behavior
(Continued)

Secondary Bondage:
What the World Calls "Addiction"
The Remedy of Last Resort

There is a major "secondary" remedy some people use in order to deal with the pain they experience when overtaken with the powerlessness of primary life pursuit apart from God. The strategy is to look for a pain reliever. To a normal thinking person, powerlessness means personal disaster. It reminds the consciousness that you have not been able to create your life. Powerlessness is excruciatingly painful, so we begin a search for something to drive away its pain, which is a reflection of not experiencing "Life." We search for something easily available that we believe will give us a sense of renewed control and will always help to drive away the pain. Some find alcohol. Some find drugs. Others find sex. The list of pain relievers is almost endless. But the bottom line is that we are looking for something to drive away the pain of the powerlessness we feel as a result of our inability to create our own life.

In the beginning, it seems as though we can control the pain reliever we have chosen. But reality keeps chasing us and, after a while, bondage begins to express itself in ways that become more and more obvious to us. And one day, we understand that we thought we could control now controls us, and we are addicted to our pain reliever. Family and friends often see it first. It is not unusual to hear them say, "He is in bondage," or "She is an addict." Then people in the outside world notice. And, as with all addictions, at some point, the addict may actually begin to see himself or herself as living in a condition of bondage and powerlessness, which is a step toward being able to break out.

The Larger Reality for All People

Unless we are walking in "Life," we are living in bondage, whether it is obvious to us or not. Most of us do not see our bondage. We are not aware of the ways in which our thinking is being conditioned by what happened to Adam and Eve and that we have many emotions which our bodies automatically generate that don't tell the truth. Very often, life becomes one gigantic, confusing, frustrating, hopeless riddle. The riddle derives from what happened to Adam and Eve, and our desperate pursuit of life apart from God. Eventually, all must run into the reality that no one except God can create or give "Life."

This is a major part of the reason so many Christian people are confused. They trusted God for their future "Life," and then, somehow, their life is not turning out the way they thought it ought to. Some give up and become depressed, and others seem to turn away from God, saying, "What's the use? I can't live right, so why should I continue to try to live right? I can't do it." To suffer without learning lessons from the suffering would be a tragedy. This final attempt to ignore those lessons and kill the pain of the reality of powerlessness is called addiction.

Some time ago, one of my clients brought in a book that focused on recovery from addiction. I perused the book and paused on a section in which the author wrote that there was no such thing as an "addictive personality." I believe it is accurate to say that psychologists, despite all of their research, have yet to identify an "addictive personality." This is because psychology cannot see the forest for the trees. Actually, there *is* such a thing as "addictive personality;" it is called a human being. It is Eden's legacy. If you have not suffered from some form of "addiction" by now, it is only by the grace of God, or else you have been in a state of denial.

When I was in school, the word "addict" was used to describe people who were addicted to alcohol or drugs. At that time, research in behavioral psychology was going on vigorously. Psychologists began to learn that people with other "habits" seemed to act just like alcoholics and drug addicts. There was a perceived need for a distinction in the definition of addiction. The two major categories of addiction were subsequently described as "process addiction" and "substance addiction." Shortly thereafter, a wider definition for addiction was proposed: "Addiction is a pathological relationship with a mood-altering experience." As a consequence of the broader definition, psychologists became able to include sex addiction, relationship addiction, romance addiction, and other kinds of addiction. We could broaden the parameters of the definition of addiction even further and say that addiction is a place where people look for life. This means we can add in addictions such as compulsive spending, one example of which is the addiction of someone who has a hobby and compulsively buys everything associated with it. Workaholism is another. A workaholic is looking for life in their work. Remember that our original statement defines addiction as bondage. Once we use this definition, we have included the whole world in it. Of course, some people who might reluctantly admit they suffer from bad habits would shun both words.

The dictionary describes an addiction simply as a bad habit. I think the word habit obscures a clear understanding of the underlying spiritual issue. The Biblical word for addiction is bondage. Bondage is a far more descriptive and meaningful word to use about what is going on. When our condition of bondage is so bad that it becomes obvious to everyone, we call this problem an addiction. Since we have already identified the addiction to power as the primary bondage, other addictions could be described as secondary bondage/addiction.

Several years ago, I developed my own definition for addiction. Here is the "Real McCoy" definition, which is not found in any text: **"Addiction is a fleshly method of attempting to cope with the pain of not experiencing abundant 'LIFE.'"**

Specific Predisposing Factors for Addiction
1. **Parental Modeling**
2. **Genetics**
3. **Peer Pressure**
4. **Chance Happenings?**

Parental Modeling

There is a variety of things that shape what we have a tendency to get addicted to. Just as parental modeling is one of the major factors that shape the power style in the expression of primary bondage; it is also a major variable that may influence the direction a person may choose for pain relief expressed in a secondary bondage/addictive process. If mom and/or dad are smokers or alcoholics, they are demonstrating, "This is the way we cope with pain in our family." However, the fact that mom and dad have certain addictions does not necessarily mean that the children are going to have the same addictions. But it does mean they are more likely to. This is because the children have had a certain type of seeking relief from pain modeled by their parents.

Genetics

A second variable relative to how a person becomes

addicted is genetics. This is expressed in a variety of ways. Increasingly, evidence suggests that some people are far more prone to becoming addicted to alcohol or morphine like substances based on their genetics. In other words, a sensitivity of their body allows them to become "locked" into addiction more quickly if they possess a genetically determined susceptibility. Their body becomes physically dependent on something more quickly than others who don't possess the same genetic susceptibility.

Another very interesting way that genetics plays a role in determining what we are more likely to become addicted to is the genetic determination of sex. I am of the school which is convinced that men and women are different in more ways than their genitalia. Men are less relationally focused. As a consequence, men are more prone to the "peculiar sin of a man," which is sex addiction. Women, being more relationally focused, are more prone to relationship sins often described as codependency or co-addiction and romance addiction.

Peer Pressure

Another factor that often influences the direction of addiction is the role of peers, especially in the teen years. This is a critical time in a person's development. A child has already had a few years to accrue pain. This is a time of increased independence and responsibility and continued exploration of new roles. If one's peers are into smokes, alcohol, or other drugs, the need to belong can be significantly manipulated by what one's peers are "into." To have a sense of acceptance, a teen may feel pressured into showing some peer conformity.

So-Called "Chance Happenings"

Certain chance experiences can lead to the exposure of a vulnerable person to a particular direction in addiction. For example, I have had more than one man tell me of finding his father's pornography or of finding pornography in some out-of-the-way place that in their mind leads them into the bondage of sex addiction. Such experiences could be described as "Chance Happenings."

The Bottom Line

Eden was a total disaster that reaches down through time and affects every person in all of his or her activities, every day, all day long. The majority of people, including most Christians, are unaware of the absolute dominating influence of Eden's disaster on how they function. Having been disconnected from their life source, Adam and Eve's most desperate need was for the "Life" that was lost. It is the basic attempt of Adam and Eve's descendants to correct this problem, in other words, to reacquire their "Life," that will be our focus in the next chapter.

Chapter Five

The Gods Must Be... Are Crazy!??

Let us return for a minute to consider our first basic riddle requiring resolution, which is the riddle of Romans 7. You will recall from our prior analysis that the speaker of Romans 7 was missing three elements:

1. **The subject is missing a "way" to be successful.**
2. **The subject is hopeless and functioning in bondage (lacks freedom).**
3. **The subject is experiencing "death," not "LIFE and Peace."**

What is the essence of these three dilemmas? What common element is missing? The essence of the deficiencies that underlie the sad lament from Romans 7 is powerlessness. The speaker is:

1. Powerless to find a way to be successful.
2. Powerless against the bondage and enslavement.
3. Powerless to create a "LIFE."

Powerlessness:
(The riddle within the riddle of Romans 7.)

It would appear that our original riddle now confronts us with a second riddle requiring resolution. The riddle within the riddle of Romans 7 is the riddle of personal powerlessness. An understanding of this riddle is the key to beginning to unlock the answer to the Romans 7 riddle. This riddle of powerlessness cannot be ignored or sidestepped. It is the key to enlightenment!

In the opening of Chapter 3, I stated that life pursuing is based on an assumed philosophy that you must have some power to be able to create or acquire your life. If you are functioning in the pursuit of life, powerlessness is the worst thing that can happen to you. It means that you are not going to be able to create, acquire, or apprehend your life! The resolution of this riddle is critical. The answer is so obvious, that the majority of the world, including Christendom, does not see it.

Adam and Eve turned away from God and began to

pursue their life apart from God in what the scripture describes as, "the way that seems right to man which leads to death." In essence, mankind began to act as if we can create our own life. We try to acquire our life through careers, marriage, children, health, hobbies, collecting things, etc. If you are religious, you may look for some life through church involvement. It is a truism that anyone who looks for something where it isn't won't find it. It follows therefore that anyone who looks for "Life" where it isn't will not find "Life." To look for something where it is not to be found is not to be in touch with reality. Not to be in touch with reality is the psychological definition of insanity. Therefore, by definition, someone who makes a practice of looking for life where it is not to be found is insane! When and where did such insanity begin?

New Age Philosophy = Old Age Insanity
Genesis 3:5 For God doth know that in the day ye eat thereof, then your eyes shall be opened, and ye shall be as gods,

This was Satan's enticement to Eve. Amazingly, her descendants have been attempting to do just that. When functioning normally, they all seem to be acting as if the creation of one's own life is a possibility. Christians are not terribly happy with the outcome of their efforts to create life. The capacity to create "Life" is indeed the work of a God. The innate insanity of Satan's lie is passed along from generation to generation of Eve's descendants. In modern times, this philosophy has been moved from hidden motivation to a place of conscious intent by those who promote what has been called "New Age Philosophy."

This holds that there is the potential to be a God in every person, and that it is the individual's responsibility to get in touch with his own internal God-like quality and unchain it to create one's own maximized life potential. This is the conscious public declaration of Satan's lie. Many Christians who would shun such obviously false philosophy would be very surprised to learn that in the sphere of their own experience, they are acting out this very insanity by acting as if they are a god that can create "Life." They have heard the gospel of good news for sinners and have trusted God for their future "Life," but are acting as if they need to create their own life for today.

What an utter tragedy it is that much of Christendom is in fact acting out the insanity of New Age philosophy in their personal experience and don't even know that they are doing it! Of course, almost no one goes around with the conscious awareness that they are trying to act like a god by trying to create their own life. It is the troubles of life's pathway that hold the potential of making our insanity apparent to us. When problems occur in those areas that we have been looking to for our life, such as marriage, career, family, etc., some begin to ask, "Why is this happening to me?" It seems as if pain is the only thing that gains the attention of a normally insane person who is acting like a god.

God permits the reality of our powerlessness to create any "Life" to begin to crush us. One of the most painful things that a life pursuing person can experience is to begin to feel powerless in some area of life pursuit. Powerlessness is the herald of disaster for the life pursuer. If you are powerless, it means you cannot create, apprehend, or acquire your life. A normal thinking person believes this is the worst thing that could possibly happen. The "Life" we all so desperately need seems beyond our reach.

I am sure that I do not need to remind you that the creation of "Life" is the business of God. It follows therefore, that humans that are attempting to usurp God's task could accurately be defined as insane or not in touch with reality. In all my years of counseling individuals, nobody has ever come to me in counseling and said, "Dr. McCoy, the reason why I am here is I have been acting like a god and I cannot stop. So I need your help to stop acting like a god." People don't consciously think like that. It is a very painful thing to learn that you are not a god! The majority of people who come to counseling are, in fact, functioning as if they are in life pursuit, and in trying to create their life through their own self-efforts, they have run into fragments of painful reality.

It is as if we have been sitting on the throne of God, and have made other things such as our spouse, career, children, etc., our gods. We have been looking to these gods to give us some life. Then, when problems occur in different areas, we cannot figure out why this is happening to us. We are trying to act as if we can create our own life. Because of His love, God permits the reality of our powerlessness to begin to crush us. Often, we think that if we could just have more of this or that, the emptiness inside of us would go away.

Long ago, Solomon wrote the ultimate dissertation on life pursuit apart from God. Solomon did everything that people aspire to do on the grandest of scales. He came from the finest family. He had the highest office in the land. He was the king. He was into power. He had 20,000 war horses in his stables. He had the largest army on the earth at that time. He was into fame. When people learned of his wisdom, they came from far countries to sit in his court. He collected wealth and was the richest man on the earth. He engaged himself in constructive work. He was a patron of the arts and sciences. He was studying the ways birds flew and boats float. He had so many servants, that he said he could create an orchestra from the children of his servants. Solomon was also probably an alcoholic and a sex addict. History records that he had 900 wives and concubines in his harem.

Solomon included the conclusions of his observations in the book of Ecclesiastes, in which he wrote, "Vanity, vanity, all is vanity." Webster says that vanity means "meaningless." The pursuit of life apart from God is meaningless. To say it another way: even if we got all that we thought would give us some life and make us happy, it would be meaningless. The painful reality of powerlessness is the wake-up call for a fortunate few who hear and respond appropriately to its message.

The Two Lessons from Communion

Jesus' disciples were arguing 1,000 years after Solomon as to which one of them was going to be greater in heaven. They couldn't figure it out, and so they had to ask Jesus directly. Jesus said that if they wanted to be great in heaven, they should become servants to other people. In other words, the only thing that anybody does in this existence that has any meaning whatsoever is to love another person, without strings attached to the relationship.

Such love requires a miracle of divine empowerment. To be able to love another person without strings attached to the relationship poses another riddle, because it is impossible for a normally functioning person to do this. Based on what happened to Adam and Eve, we cannot give this kind of love. There is not one man or woman on this planet who has the power within himself or herself to love another person in a God-honoring fashion. It is not natural to love without attaching strings. The greatest challenge of life is to learn how to love another person in a God-honoring way and thus do something meaningful. This is why spouses give us such a wonderful opportunity to learn how to love another person.

I argue for the right of people to set any goals they wish. I think the critical question is, "Do you want your goals to be meaningful?" If you want your goals to be meaningful, that will involve serving others. Loving and serving others in a way that honors God is something that has to be learned. It is not natural. (What the Bible calls "natural affection" is love with strings attached.) So those who are married and feel their spouses are millstones must learn that their spouses present an opportunity to learn to love and serve. Doing something meaningful involves learning how to love people who sometimes act in an unsavory manner. That is where the real challenge comes in. We need a miracle of divine empowerment to carry this off. A "normal thinking," "life pursuing" person cannot carry this off. (Jesus said, "Without me ye can do nothing" John 15:5.)

How do you love a person who is unsavory? Loving unsavory people is not natural. The natural is, "I will love you if you love me back." Unsavory people do not often love back. Yet we are supposed to love them. Doing that requires a miracle and is another apparent riddle. Part of that riddle will be answered more completely when we look at the riddle of the Christian's abundant "Life."

If you have all of "Life" already, and are totally secure, then you can be free from this desperate pursuit of life and free to turn your attention to others. You can then be concerned about *their* welfare and learn how to love them freely, because you already have your "Life" and it is completely secure.

CHAPTER 6

The Riddle of the Christians' Abundant "LIFE"

Perhaps one of the greatest riddles of all for Christians is the riddle of their abundant "Life." Evangelicals are correct to warn everyone of the necessity of being reconciled to God. Most folks believe the "Gospel of good news" is accompanied by the promise of a future "Life" with God, which will be entered into upon death, or the rapture of the church. Contrary to popular opinion, abundant "Life" begins when you receive it! This is a great mystery in Christendom. I have asked numerous evangelical pastors of many denominations the question, "During your seminary training did you have a class on what abundant 'Life' is?" No one has responded in the affirmative!

Since this glorious reality is not being taught in most institutions of higher learning, it is no surprise that it is not being taught from most pulpits. Instead, Christians are told more and more things to do and urged to try harder in their walk. Some are presented substitutes for spirituality. The three major substitutes for spirituality in the church today are legalism, experiences, and the pursuit of the knowledge of doctrine.

The scripture makes it clear that the believer in Christ's substitutionary death has been given all of "Life" at the moment of faith. That "Life" is completely secure. The believer has been made rich beyond his capacity to imagine or grasp. Christians possess all of this because they are the object of the love of a God whose very essence is love. It follows that a person walking in such a "Life" has an antidote for feelings that are attempting to deprive him of the experience of "Life" and peace. ("The TRUTH shall set you free!")

The Major Problem: Normal Thinking

Almost everyone who shows up in a counseling office is there because they have been acting and thinking normally about life. They are operating in the "way that seems right," which according to Proverbs 16 leads to the experience of death. People do not come to counseling because of the "Life" they are experiencing. They come to counseling because of the death they are experiencing! Normal thinking people are in "life pursuit" and are dedicated to three people: me, myself, and I. Normal thinking people are acting as if life is a "do-it-yourself" creative activity, and it's not going well. Normal thinking people are also functioning as if they believe that life comes in degrees of life, and if some person or circumstance would change, then they might be able to acquire or apprehend just a little more of life.

Reality: "LIFE" is not a Matter of Degree!

"Life" is all or none. A person either has all of "Life" or he does not have "Life" at all. When a person trusts Christ, he gets the whole package of "Life." "Life" can be likened to white light. When you pass a ray of white light through a prism and onto a piece of white paper, you can see all the colors of the rainbow on the paper. "Life" is like white light in that "Life" is composed of a whole series of constituent elements that taken together make up "Life." A person cannot be half-alive. When a person receives Christ, he receives the whole "Life" package. All the constituent elements that make up "Life" become the possession of the believer at the moment of faith. Any feeling he or she is experiencing that seeks to deny this reality is a lie. A normal thinking person is functioning as if the "way that seems right" is in fact reality.

> *2 Corinthians 5:17   Therefore if any man be in Christ, he is a new creature: old things are passed away; behold, all things are become new.*

All the offspring of Adam and Eve are so absolutely and fundamentally flawed that God himself cannot repair us. It was necessary to make us new creations. He has chosen to leave this new creation in the same body where the flesh resides and is on default. This sets up the conflict described in Romans 7. If the Christian has been made a new creation and has been given abundant "Life," what is it, and how do you make it your experience? We want to talk about this because it is the basis of understanding the three riddles under consideration in this book. The last lament of the person quoted in Romans 7 is, *"Who will deliver me from the body of this death."* Obviously, this is a person who is not experiencing abundant "Life."

It is really important for Christians to understand that God has not only provided them a future "Life," but He has also provided them "Life" for today! This is true irrespective of any circumstance! 2 Corinthians 5:17 says, *"Therefore if any man be in Christ, he is a new creature: old things are passed away; behold, all things are become new."* So what *are* these new elements of life that people receive when they become a Christian?

The Elements Of Life: Identity

1 John 3:1 Behold, what manner of love the Father hath bestowed upon us, that we should be called the sons of God:

The first "Life" element that I would like to talk about is one of the most important, because it is foundational to all the others. This is the "Life" element of our identity, which relates directly to our intrinsic worth, which is the basis of self-esteem. When a person becomes a Christian, God the Father confers upon them a new identity. If I were to ask you, "What is your identity as a Christian?" I wonder what you would tell me. Some will correctly say, "I am a child of God." Most Christians know that they are children of God. In fact, when I was a child, I memorized a verse that spoke of that. John 1:12 says, **"But as many as received him, to them gave he the power to become the sons of God."**

For many years, I have known that I was a child of God, but it really never impacted my life very much. The Bible makes it very clear that man and God are not alone in the universe. There are all kinds of other beings in the universe of diverse forms and functions called angels. In my years of ignorance, my concept of what it meant to be a child of God was to be a faceless member in the multitude of the heavenly hosts. Yes, I was going to be in heaven and enjoy the wonders of heaven; but I am just kind of a nobody amongst all the millions and/or trillions (?) of beings who are living in heaven.

One day, however, I began reading the book of Hebrews, specifically the first chapter, where it says, "To which of the angels said he at any time, I will be to him a father and he will be to me a son?" Then at the end of the first chapter it says, concerning the angels, *"Are they not all ministering spirits sent forth to minister to those who be the heirs of salvation."* (Heb. 1:14) All of a sudden, a light went on in my head. To be a child of God is to be raised in rank and station above all the other beings in the universe, to become a member of God's royal family. It is the highest office of the universe, save only that of God himself. In fact, the Bible states that Christians become members of the body of Christ, which to me, sounds like we are becoming a total, everlasting unity with Deity. That whole conception of this new identity with Deity absolutely boggles my mind.

Satan, the devil, is described in the Old Testament as the embodiment of knowledge and beauty, before he fell. Lucifer (Satan) is the chief prince of the chief princes of the angelic forms. He is an incredible being with incredible powers. Yet, if we were going to draw a celestial corporate chart, we would have God as the head of the family. Then there are the children of God, and there is the royal butler, who is Lucifer, the chief of the servant forms. That is his place on a celestial chart, since he is an angel form. Remember, the original parents of human beings were made in the image of God. That is a very different birthright, if you please. Satan's birthright was to be created in the image of a servant. This is a very different place and position.

Who is the most famous child of God? Of course, that would be Christ. It follows then that if you are the possessor of "Life," then you are the brother or sister of the One who created the Universe. What an awesome identity! Our identity relates to our intrinsic worth, which is not something that you or I create. We don't have anything to do with it. A Father Creator confers intrinsic worth. And He has given us the intrinsic worth to be children of God. This is the highest intrinsic worth there can possibly be, and is directly connected to our self-esteem, which is usually mirrored to us initially in our family of origin. Then we build on that, depending upon our successes in life, and whether or not we are surrounded by people who say we are wonderful. But if we do not have a lot of success, and if the people around us say we are not lovely, then our self-esteem goes up and down depending on the winds of circumstance. And if the circumstances are great, we can have good self-esteem. If our circumstances are bad; if, for example, our spouse says we are terrible, our self-esteem can be devastated. Self-esteem, really, needs to be rooted in intrinsic worth. We cannot add to nor can we subtract from our intrinsic worth through our behavior. Every person who is a Christian, who has been given "Life" and this new identity, has a right to a good self-esteem. Self-esteem needs to be rooted in our identity.

Inheritance

Let us move on to discuss another gift, a second life element, which is our inheritance. Ephesians chapter 1 says, "It pleased the father to give us an inheritance." The inheritance that has been given to us is commensurate with the rank and station to which we have been raised.

Ephesians 1:3 Blessed be the God and Father of our Lord Jesus Christ, who hath blessed us with all spiritual blessings in heavenly places in Christ:

Everything that is worthwhile, that lasts forever, is already in our account. It is in our inheritance. Every Christian has been made rich in a manner beyond comprehending!

Romans 8:32 He that spared not his own Son, but delivered him up for us all, how shall he not with him also freely give us all things?

If the Father did not spare Christ in his plan to redeem us to Himself, if He did not withhold His most precious Son, then He is not going to withhold anything from us that is worthwhile and lasts forever. Our inheritance is absolutely incredible.

Romans 8:17 and if children, then heirs; heirs of God, and joint-heirs with Christ;

Another verse says that Christ is the heir of all things. We are talking about wealth off the scale. When Paul wrote of the people in the book of Corinthians, he wrote of them as being monetarily poor but possessing everything.

> **2 Corinthians 6:10b** *...as having nothing, and yet possessing all things.*

Our conception of wealth in this existence is really limited. When we think of our riches, we usually think of worldly things. In this existence, for example, people kill for gold. But gold is nothing more than lead with a few more particles running around the nucleus. In this existence, physicists use lead to screen out atomic rays. Gold would be better, but it is too expensive to use for that purpose. The scriptures state that in the heavenly city gold is so common, it is used to pave the streets. But it is a funny kind of gold. It is a transparent gold, which lets the light rays through. It is hard to comprehend somebody wanting to sneak out into the street to steal a cobblestone. The whole conception of what wealth is, what we understand here, is so different from what it is going to be in heaven.

So, this wealth that we have is just incredible. An English author wrote a book called, "A Brief History of Time." He holds the chair of theoretical physics at Cambridge University, and he is not a Christian. In his book, he postulates that taking a point and stretching it in all directions created the universe.

I do not know if he is right or not, but it is totally consistent with the scriptures, because the scriptures state that the things which are unseen are more real than the things which are made. The room in which you may be reading this contains an infinite number of points. If the author is correct, we have a brother (Christ), who can take a point and stretch it apart in all directions and make a universe. This is just mind-boggling to me. All people who have been reconciled to God have been given an inheritance, which is commensurate with the station to which they have been raised. Every Christian is rich in a fashion which they cannot comprehend.

1 Corinthians 2: 9,10a But as it is written, Eye hath not seen, nor ear heard, neither have entered into the heart of man, the things which God hath prepared for them that love him. But God hath revealed them unto us by his Spirit.

We are discussing the things that have been revealed. Just this little bit is like getting a peek through a doorway into another room. In the other room are the most incredible things. We are given just a little hint about what is ahead. But we are children of God now. Our inheritance has already been set aside.

Here are some other "Life" elements in our "Life" package.

Acceptability

Ephesians 1:6 to the praise of the glory of his grace, wherein he hath made us accepted in the beloved.

The writer of Ephesians says that God has made us acceptable. We are acceptable in Christ. When He made us new creations, He made us **completely acceptable**. Let a nut represent a person: God has made the essential essence of the nut acceptable. But God has chosen to leave this new essential essence inside the old shell, the flesh. Consequently, I sometimes act unacceptably. My unacceptable behavior is not derived from the new creation, because that is the nature of God. My unacceptable behavior occurs because of the shell; the flesh, not the new creation, is in control of me. But the essential essence of what I am remains acceptable.

Acceptability is an area of pain where so many people struggle. If a spouse in some manner communicates, "You are unacceptable," it feels like they may be right. But if we have the "Life" of Christ, God has made us acceptable. If our behavior is unacceptable, then we need to correct our behavior. Our intrinsic acceptability does not change. I remember a group in which men were discussing some recent experiences. One man was describing his wife, and said he was trying so hard to make his wife accept him. After he talked, another man spoke about trying so hard in his work. But no matter what he did, the people at work continued to criticize his behavior.

At the end of the hour, I asked these Christian men, "How many men in this room are acceptable?" Immediately, a man looked at me and said, "To whom?" I said, "That was not the question. My question was, 'How many of you are acceptable?'? If you are acceptable, then to who is irrelevant?" Is that logical? Do you understand what I am saying? These were Christian men being told that they were unacceptable. They were beginning to feel unacceptable. They did not really comprehend the fact that people can reject us, but that does not change our underlying acceptability, because God has made us acceptable.

You cannot go to counseling to make yourself acceptable. You cannot change yourself to make yourself acceptable. You cannot pull yourself off the floor by your own bootstraps to make yourself acceptable. God has already made us acceptable. And He is waiting for us to walk around in this wonderful gift that He has given us. It is part of the "Life" package.

Most folks who are married and thinking normally are looking to their spouses to have a sense of being acceptable. In reality, they are looking to their spouses for acceptability instead of looking to God. All a spouse can do is to tell us how acceptable we are to them at the moment. Only God has the capacity to make us acceptable at all times. Since acceptability is a "Life" element that only comes from God, the action of looking to ones wife for intrinsic acceptability represents a violation of the first commandment and represents worshiping the creature more than the Creator, God!

Wholeness

Col 2:10 and ye are complete in him, which is the head of all principality and power:

When God makes us a new creation in Christ, He does not leave off any parts. The metaphor of the newborn baby comes to mind. When a baby is born, the baby has all his parts, but he is just a baby. The baby needs to continue to grow, so that his parts become stronger and more functional. When God makes us a new creation, He does not leave off any parts. He creates us as a whole person. Over the years, I have met multitudes of people who arrive at adulthood with a sense that they don't measure up. They feel they must work more or strive harder to be okay. They sense that they fall just short, are incomplete, and are missing some necessary element required for success. The good news for those who have "Life" is that when God made you a new creation he didn't leave off any parts. Not only were you made acceptable, you were also made whole!

Total Forgiveness

Colossians 2:13 and you, being dead in your sins and the uncircumcision of your flesh, hath he quickened together with him, having forgiven you all trespasses;

Let's begin by acknowledging that there is much conflict in evangelical Christendom over this subject. Space does not allow us to review the pros and cons of the conflicting arguments. I shall just discuss what I believe is true. First, let me state that "all" is not all unless it *is* all! Some folks are worried about putting an emphasis on this, because people might feel that it could be understood as being cheap grace, which means, "If you want to do it, well, why not do it, because it is all forgiven anyway." That is not the purpose of this revelation.

This understanding is given so that we could have a sense of how much God loves us. After decades of normal thinking and looking for my life "in the way that seemed right," I had an epiphany. I realized that every second I look for my life in some place other than where "Life" comes from, I am sinning. In reality, my sins are as the sands of the sea and God has forgiven me all of them. This, to me, is an incredible measure or yardstick of God's love for me, to forgive me all my trespasses. If we were not forgiven all our sins, there would be no humans in heaven!

The concept of total forgiveness is a hard one for many of us to grasp, especially if we are operating in that carnal mindset. The carnal mind has two other strategies that we often get into before we are willing to listen to the truth regarding our forgiveness. These two strategies are God-dishonoring. Some of us get into self-punishment programs. We do something wrong and when feel guilty, we begin to internally self-punish, which is God-dishonoring, because Christ suffered for our sins. And God does not want us to punish ourselves. What he wants for us is a transformed life. He wants us to enter into the experience of "Life." Others of us get into what I call self-improvement programs. We say to ourselves, "Okay, I screwed up. Now I am going to improve myself so that I will not have to feel as guilty."

That is equally impossible, like bending over to the floor, picking yourself up by your shoes, and trying to pull yourself off the floor. It cannot be done. The improvements that we require are found in the "Life" elements that I am talking about. God did the cleanup program when He made us new creations. We cannot improve what God has done. God wants us to walk around in His improvement. He is waiting for us to do that. Most of us are so caught up in life pursuit, in making our own life and our own agendas, that we miss out on this wonderful gift. In fact, we often do not even know we have it, because we are so busy looking for it elsewhere.

Power (Enablement)

2 Timothy 1:7 For God hath not given us the spirit of fear; but of power

The reason why God's power is so important is because it is the antidote to our powerlessness. In other words, we do not have the power to create any "Life" at all, but that is what we are trying to do when we are thinking normally. God has the power. And if we are going to live in a God-honoring way, we require His divine empowerment. This is such a critical element: power to deal with our life in a way that honors God. It is necessary for us to get connected with this power. This power is what Jesus was talking about when He said, *"I am the vine, ye are the branches: He that abideth in me, and I in him, the same bringeth forth much fruit: for without me ye can do nothing…"* (John 15: 5) In other words, He is saying you must stay connected to the power source so that you can provide a solution to the problem of Romans 7: being unable to do what you should do, and being unable to stop doing what you know you ought to stop doing.

Love

Love is a key "Life" element that is all-encompassing. The Bible states that the very essence of the character of God is LOVE and that love is directed towards us (His children).

1 John 4:8b for God is love

Ephesians 2:4 But God, who is rich in mercy, for his great love wherewith he loved us,

The gift of "Life" that we have been given by God is an expression of that love in its entirety.

2 Timothy 1: 7 For God hath not given us the spirit of fear; but of power, and of <u>love</u>,

I personally believe that what really motivates anybody to want to serve God is getting a very clear picture of how much God loves them. I think that is the only thing that transforms us to an attitude of wanting to serve God. In fact, John says, we love Him because he first loved us. I can recall in the early days, when I was 11 and I heard the gospel of good news for sinners that God actually died for me and I was reconciled to Him so I could have my sins forgiven and have a pass into heaven. I was awed that God could love me like that-- He would love me that much! As large as that is, and as necessary as that is, and as wonderful as that is, those things are just a tiny part of the package. We have received the whole package of "Life." **God is for us!** He has not only purposed to reconcile us to Himself, and to forgive our sins, but He has also called us to be his children. My greatest desire and purpose of writing this book would be that the reader would take away an enlarged understanding of how much God loves us by gifting us with the entire "Life" package. Our motivation to serve God is in direct correlation to our understanding of God's love for us.

*** 1 John 4:19 We love him,
because he first loved us.***

Because of His love for us, God comes to us first and gifts us with these elements of his love. He gifts us with his "Life," which is ours in the here and now. This is exciting!

I have often tried to imagine a neat situation for me that would be larger than the one that I have been describing. I have tried to figure out if there is something that could be greater. I have been able to come up with only one thing. That would be for Claude McCoy and the Holy Father to exchange places. That is the only thing that I can conceive of which would be greater than the "Life" gift that God has provided. Actually, this is unnecessary, because the scripture states that all Christians are joint heirs with Christ to the throne of the universe. We are heirs of God and joint heirs with Christ. Having the Father and me exchange places is unnecessary. We are discussing a love that is absolutely incomprehensible. The apostle Paul, in one of his letters, wanted us to know about the length and the breadth, and the height and the depth of God's love. God's love is gifted to everyone who will receive it.

Revelation 22:17 And whosoever will, let him take the water of life freely.

God takes us from insanity, which is rebelling against Him, and transforms us into visions of loveliness. He has called us to be members of His royal family. David wrote a Psalm in which he says, "God is for me." (Psalm 56:9) The heartbeat of the universe is for His children, and He has purposed to communicate to them everything. This is His abundant "Life." There is no greater love. God cannot love his children more.

When I started out my early Christian life, I determined that I was going to be a successful Christian. And the reason why I wanted to do that is to have God to love me more. I wanted to get Him to accept me more, because I was going to do this good job for Him. Was that ever a bunch of confusion and faulty thinking? God cannot love his children more, because He has already gifted them with "Life." There is no greater love. The greatest love that is, we already have.

Sound Mind

2 Timothy 1:7 For God hath not given us the spirit of fear; but of power, and of love, and of a sound mind.

Some Bible versions translate this as "disciplined thinking." Earlier in the book, we discussed how Adam and Eve's thinking was changed as a result of their disobedience, when they began to operate with a mindset that the Bible calls carnal or fleshly.

Romans 8:7 Because the carnal mind is enmity against God: for it is not subject to the law of God, neither indeed can be.

Adam and Eve began to pursue their life apart from God in a way that seems right to man but leads to death. To look for something where it isn't, is to be out of touch with reality. Psychology experts say that if you are not in touch with reality, you are insane. To think normally is to function in insanity. Sound-mindedness is a gift to be found in our "Life" package. If I am operating with the mind of Christ, I am sane, because God is not crazy. If I am thinking normally, I am thinking carnally. This means I am in life pursuit, and I am not in touch with reality. This gift of God is given so we can walk sanely, and think sanely in an insane world. It is an incredible necessary gift. Our daily problem is that our carnal mind is on default and functions automatically, unless we take a conscious and deliberate action to assert the truth.

Righteousness And Holiness

1 Corinthians 1:30 But of him are ye in Christ Jesus, who of God is made unto us wisdom, and righteousness, and sanctification, and redemption:

Ephesians 4:24 And that ye put on the new man, which after God is created in righteousness and true holiness.

Two elements of "Life" that we do not ordinarily think about in everyday life are righteousness and holiness. We are going to need these elements if we are going to exist in the presence of the Holy God and survive. So, if we are going to exist and survive in his presence, we must be righteous and holy. God gifts us with these elements because there is no other way we can acquire them. He gives us His righteousness and holiness! If you are a Christian you have these "Life" elements today!

Fellowship

1 John 1:4 and these things write we unto you, that your joy may be full.

In this passage, John is speaking of two things which are intrinsic to the experience of joy. One is fellowship with the Holy Father. The second is fellowship with other members of the royal family of God. It just boggles my mind that I can say that the King of Kings and Lord of Lords is my Father. He is yours also, if you possess "Life." After addressing fellowship with the Father, John speaks of fellowship with the other brothers and sisters of the royal family. In this life, we get only a taste of what that fellowship will be like. We get a taste of it in healthy marriages and in friendship. But in this existence, there are many impediments to fellowship that God, in His wisdom, has placed there. Time is an impediment. For example, I cannot fellowship with somebody who lived in 1492. Language is another impediment. I do not speak Swahili, so if you were Swahili, I could not talk with you. One's sex and marital status also limits us in this area of fellowship.

All of these impediments are going to be done away with in the future. Time is going to be done away with. We will all be speaking one language. The Bible states that there is neither marriage nor giving in marriage in the future. We are going to enter into an incredible fellowship with brothers and sisters, which in this world we hardly get a taste of. I am really looking forward to that. The fellowship of the future is going to be from totally pure hearts and pure motivation. It is going to be very different from what we have here and now.

Security

The last LIFE element I want to talk about is security. The Christian has been given every form of security. I am not going to take the time to talk about all the verses, because there are so many, but let me just take a couple of them. One is security to be found in all circumstances.

Romans 8: 28 and we know that all things work together for good to them that love God, to them who are the called according to his purpose.

God has the power to cause some good thing to come out of any circumstances or any tragedy. I believe God often allows us to experience difficulties so that we can get it straight in our mind about where our "Life" comes from. Take the example of a parent who loses a child. If the parents have been looking for their life in that child, it feels like they have lost part of their life. They have in fact suffered a terrible loss, but not of "Life." God can make good come out of all these tragedies. We all need to get it straight in our mind where our 'Life' comes from. We also need to understand about our powerlessness. This is such an incredibly important lesson to learn. I think this is a common good that God can bring to us from many such circumstances.

We are secure in God's love.

Romans 8:38, 39 For I am persuaded, that neither death, nor life, nor angels, nor principalities, nor powers, nor things present, nor

> *things to come, Nor height, nor depth, nor any other creature, shall be able to separate us from the love of God, which is in Christ Jesus our Lord.*

There is security from the condemnatory accusation of others.

> ***Romans 8:33a Who shall lay anything to the charge of God's elect?***

There are other forms of security as well, but I am not going to take the time to describe them all.

Let us reflect further on the "Life" elements we have identified. The identity that God has conferred upon us ought to have a bearing on our self-esteem. The fact that God has made us acceptable ought to have a bearing on our need for acceptance. The fact that God has made us complete in Christ ought to have a bearing on our need for wholeness. The fact that He has totally forgiven us ought to have a bearing on our guilt when we fail. The fact that His power is available to us ought to have a bearing on our powerlessness. The fact that He loves us ought to have a bearing on our need for love. His sound-mindedness ought to have a bearing on our natural problem of functioning with a sound mind.

We have assembled a list of "Life" elements. There is something for every single need we have as a human being. Taken together: Abundant "Life." Christ is the only "Life" that any person has. If you have "Life," it is Christ. Paul said, *"For me to live is Christ."* He said, *"I can do all things through Christ who strengthens me."* In Colossians 2, he says, *"When Christ, who is our life, shall appear…"* And when Jesus Himself was here, He said, *"I am the way, the truth and the life."* That is the missing answer to the riddle of Romans 7. The person in Romans 7 is operating in a way that seems right to a man that leads to death. He is not operating in Christ as the way; he is operating in his own way. Jesus said, *"I am the truth,"* and he said, *"You shall know the truth, and the truth shall set you free."* Free from what? Bondage. What bondage? The bondage to the fear of death, i.e., the fear that you will not be able to create, acquire, or apprehend your life.

> *Hebrews 2: 15 And deliver them who through fear of death were all their lifetime subject to bondage.*

The last thing Christ said was, "I am the LIFE." We have been documenting "Life" elements. This is what is missing in the testimony of Romans 7. This is the problem of a person who is trying to do something that they know they should do and cannot do it, or is trying to stop something that they know they should stop. They are missing the three elements. They are missing Christ as the way. They are missing Christ as the truth that sets them free from the bondage of the fear of death, i.e., that they are not going to get their life. And they are missing the experience of the abundant "Life."

CHAPTER 7

The Process of Laying Hold of "LIFE"

Step One: Knowledge

I received the "Life" package when I was 11 years old. I was unaware that there was a process involved in experiencing "Life." The first step in the process of laying hold of "Life" is knowledge. The scripture says, *"My people perish for lack of knowledge."* In 2 Peter 1, Peter gives another succinct formula for successful Christian life. He starts out by talking about salvation. He says, *"Whereby are given unto us exceeding great and precious promises, that by these we become partakers of the divine nature. Now add to this..."* The second word out of his mouth is knowledge. Every Christian needs to know clearly where "Life" comes from, what "Life" is, and how you make "Life" your experience. Without that knowledge, it is difficult to get started on a successful Christian walk because when you are thinking normally, you are in life pursuit, operating in a way that seems right to a man, and you cannot get out of it without the knowledge of the Truth that sets you free.

Step Two: Faith

The second step in the process of laying hold of "Life" is faith.

In Romans 5: 2 By whom also we have access by faith into this grace wherein we stand,

It is not enough for me to know that I am a child of God. If I do not believe it, then I cannot access the self-esteem that I have a right to, based on my identity in Christ. So faith is a necessary element. It opens the door to "Life." Every Christian has just enough faith, because God gave him just enough faith to reckon that Christ died for their sins. Therefore, Christians have this same faith, which is just enough to reckon that these other wonderful things are true also.

Step Three: Transformation Through Application

The third step, Paul talks about that in Romans 12:2. I call it the application step.

Romans 12:2 and be not conformed to this world: but be ye transformed by the renewing of your mind

I must bring into conscious awareness these elements of "Life" as they relate to my problems. I must believe God and act accordingly in the face of feelings that are trying to drive me in an opposite, crazy direction.

The reason why Paul tells us not to be like the rest of the world is because the rest of the world is crazy. The reason why he tells us not to be like the rest of the world is because the rest of the world is looking in the wrong place for their "Life." It is the insanity of looking for "Life" where it is not. Paul is saying we should not be like people who are looking for their "Life" where it isn't. We need to remind ourselves of the **"Life"** elements which we possess that relate to our problems. WE NEED TO BELIEVE THE TRUTH AND THEN ACT ACCORDINGLY.

The reason why most of us call something a problem is because it feels as if the problem is threatening our life in some way. That is why we call something a problem. The problem may be making us feel insecure. The problem may be making us feel unloved. It may be making us feel like we are incomplete or some element of life seems to be threatened. In reality, this is an illusion, because the scripture states that the Christian's "Life" is hid with Christ in God. It may certainly seem to us that this problem *is* threatening our life, but, of course, that cannot be happening. So we need to remind ourselves of the "Life" we have that relates to the problem. And we need to believe God and act accordingly in the face of the feelings that we are experiencing which are telling us something else.

I was in the Navy during the Korean War. In boot camp, I was taught how to perform sentry duty. There were 10 rules of a sentry that I had to memorize. The first rule of a sentry was, "I will walk my post in a military manner, keeping always on the alert." Many of us function in an unconscious and reactive mode, rather than a conscious and deliberate mode. We function in our mind as if there is no objective observer armed with the Truth whose task is to monitor our thoughts and feelings. What we need to do is function as if there is a sentry on duty at the doorway of the mind who is going to walk his post in a military manner, keeping always on the alert. His task is an ongoing, objective assessment of the thoughts and feelings that are coming into the mind.

Another rule of the sentry was that if somebody

approached, you hail him or her with, "Halt, who goes there?" And the next rule says if they do not identify themselves, you start shooting. However, if they identify themselves, you say, "Advance and be recognized." In this same way, there needs to be a sentry on duty in our mind who will assess all our thoughts and feelings that are seeking entry and compare them with the TRUTH that sets us free. Are they the truth? Is this reality? Spiritual battles are won or lost at the threshold of the mind. Almost every negative feeling that a Christian experiences does not tell the truth. If a person does not know what the TRUTH is, the false thoughts and negative feelings will take him hostage.

To put this another way, we need to practice "mindfulness." Mindfulness involves a conscious and deliberate monitoring and assessment of all thoughts and feelings seeking access to the doorway of our minds. To reiterate, spiritual battles are won or lost at the doorway to the mind. The sentry on duty at that door needs to be armed with the Truth that sets us free. Everything needs to be examined by the Truth, and responsive decisions must be made by consciously and deliberately asserting the Truth. If the thoughts and feelings agree with the Truth, we must give God thanks. If the thoughts and feelings disagree with the

Truth, however, then we need to reckon ourselves dead to them. Active, deliberate, conscious mindfulness is critical to success. If a person is not consciously functioning with the mind of Christ, they are a lost battle just waiting to happen!

The Fourth Step: The Walk

Wouldn't it be wonderful if all we had to do was learn the Truth, believe it and apply it once, and then live happy ever after? Our journey here does not work that way, because Christians are called to a walk. A walk does not consist of one step. Rather, a walk involves taking step after step after step. Honoring God in the morning does not take care of the afternoon or the evening.

Let us consider the mechanics of our bodies when we walk. When we wish to go somewhere, we stand and throw our weight off balance and have faith that one of our legs is going to come out and keep us from falling on the floor. We continue to throw our weight off balance and have faith that the other leg is going to come out and keep us from falling. In fact, every step we take becomes an act of faith that we are going to get to our destination.

A successful walk requires commitment over time. Commitment is fueled by motivation. The motivation of which I speak is directly correlated with the measure of comprehension a person has as to how much God loves them. My greatest desire in writing this book is that you would acquire an enlarged understanding as to how much God loves you and has demonstrated that love by gifting you with LIFE.

We Love God Because He First Loved Us

The scripture is clear that we love God because He first loved us. Our understanding of the height and depth, length and breadth of God's love for us illuminates the scope of His love which, if we make it ours, leads us to respond to Jesus' command, "If you love me love one another"! This love internalized is the genesis and force of our commitment to respond to Christ's command and to endure troubles over time.

Let us pretend for a minute that I have a problem and I tell you about my problem. As soon as I tell you about my problem, there are a whole bunch of things you know about me that I did not tell you. The first thing you know is that I am feeling inadequate. If I felt adequate, I would deal with the problem and probably would not even discuss it with you. The second thing you know is that I am feeling incomplete, because I am feeling as if I am missing what it takes to be adequate. And, since I am feeling inadequate and incomplete, I am probably feeling unacceptable as well, because it is unacceptable to be in a position not to be able to deal with my life. If I am feeling inadequate, incomplete, and unacceptable, I probably have a self-esteem problem.

By the way, is that the kind of person you would normally be attracted to, i.e., someone who is inadequate, feeling incomplete, and has self-esteem problems. No? I am already feeling unlovely, and now you have told me that I am unlovely because I have told you about my problem. Now I am beginning to feel even more unlovely. I believe that if I feel unlovely and you think I am unlovely, then I must be unlovely. But this is not true. So what is the point of all this? It is my first point: "Life" is all or none. If I have got a problem, it appears as if it is affecting a hunk of my entire life.

Now, let us pretend I just learned about my "Life" in Christ, and I am determined to apply the principles of the scriptures to my life in a practical way, so I am all excited. I then head home from my office and run into a problem. I begin to experience all those things I just talked to you about. Question: How many of those emotions are telling me the truth about my circumstances? Answer: None of them. Almost every negative emotion that a Christian experiences does not tell the truth. But if you do not know what the Truth is, you cannot effectively process those emotions. If there were nobody on duty checking out what you are experiencing and comparing it with the Truth, there would be no way to sort things out. Paul admonishes us to bring every thought into captivity to Christ

2 Corinthians 10:5 Casting down imaginations, and every high thing that exalteth itself against the knowledge of God, and bringing into captivity every thought to the obedience of Christ;

I would remind you that during wartime, sentries could be court-martialed and sometimes executed for going to sleep on watch. As Christians, we are in fact involved in spiritual warfare.

In conclusion, we started out talking about riddles that require resolution. We talked about the person of Romans 7 who knew what to do but was not doing it, knew what not to do, and could not stop, and was experiencing death. We have also taken a look at powerlessness which is the riddle embedded in Romans 7. The Romans 7 person is operating in his or her own way, the way that seems right to man that leads to death. The person of Romans 7 is operating in bondage to the fear of death, the fear that he or she is not going to get a life. When Jesus was here, He said, "I am the way, the Truth, and the LIFE." He subsequently said you shall know the Truth and the Truth shall set you free from this bondage of the fear of death. These are the missing elements in Romans 7 and the lament of the person in Romans 7.

The good news is that all those who have been reconciled to God have had their sins forgiven and have been given all of "Life." The sad news is that most Christian folks do not know about it. I call it the "Gospel of good news for Christians." That is why it is such a privilege to share this wonderful truth.

I reiterate that what really motivates anybody to want to serve God is getting a very clear picture of how much God loves them. When I was 11 and heard the gospel of good news for sinners, I was awed. I learned that God actually died for me, to reconcile me to Him and to forgive my sins. As a consequence of my trust in Christ, heaven for me was assured.

As large and necessary and wonderful as salvation and reconciliation are, they are just a tiny part of God's love package. Christians have the whole package. God is for us. He has purposed not only to reconcile us to Him and to forgive our sins, but He has also called us to be His children and made us His heirs and joint heirs with Christ. He has given us His

"Life" to live out today. By appropriating that "Life," we can put the troubles and trials of this journey into perspective and honor God in the process.

Armed with your new understanding of your "Life" in Christ we can now assess what was going on in the Chapter 1 stories of Christians in trouble. All of the troubled Christian persons described in the stories were:

1. Functioning as if life is a matter of degree and they need more degrees.
2. Looking in the wrong place for their life.
3. Thinking normally, "naturally", "carnally".
4. Functioning in bondage to the fear that they are not going to be able to create or fully acquire their life.
5. Delusional.
6. Acting as if life is a do it yourself project.
7, Failing to connect the "Life" that they already possess to the circumstances that they are going through.
9. Blind to the reality that they already possess all of "Life".
10. Acting as if they are a god who can create his/her own life.
11. Violating the First Commandment

12. Operating with idolatrous thinking, i.e. looking to someone or something other than God for his/her" Life".
13. Hostage to lying emotions.
14. Either ignorant of or rebellious to the truth of what Christ meant when he said he was the Way, the Truth, and the "Life".
15. Experiencing death and not "Life" and peace.
16. Not "abiding" in the power source that could have enabled their success.

CHAPTER 8

Tips From the Counseling Office

This book was not written to teach counseling methodology. It is about practical theology. It was written to clarify and to underscore the delusion that underlies most of the issues for which people seek counseling. Unless the basic life issue (delusion) has been addressed, other counseling is not likely to have a God-approved outcome. Counseling that does not address the life issue pushes persons further and further into the bondage of Romans Chapter 7. They may know more and more about how to communicate or how to resolve conflicts, but they can't implement what they have learned because they continue to look in the wrong places for their "Life."

If my Christian patients are open to it, I teach them what I have described in this book. I then give them a homework assignment, which focuses on the implementation of what they have learned. They are instructed that if significant problems occur between our visits, they are to answer four questions in writing and to bring back to our sessions any questions that might arise out of answering the four questions. Each person is given two sheets of paper.

One sheet contains the following four questions:

1 a. What is the problem?

1 b. What is the problem, specifically?

(Remember, we think something is a problem because it feels as if it is threatening some element of our "Life" when, in reality, this is never happening)

2. How are you responding to the problem?

3. What does the Bible say about this problem and references?

4. What further steps must you take to rectify the problem if any?

The second sheet is a help sheet with a list of "Life" elements and scriptural references pertaining to each element. First, clients are instructed to make a general statement describing the problem they are experiencing and cautioned to describe their own problem not someone else's. Next, they are to consult the help sheet and determine which life element/elements seem to be threatened by the problem. (Remember that in reality. their "Life" is never under threat.) Fourth, they are to describe how they are handling the problem. Last, they are to go back to their "help" sheet and write down the scriptural references, which they identified in their 1 b. analysis. The answer to the fourth step always should begin in the same manner. It goes something like this: "I need to remind myself of those elements of life that I have been given from God and are not under any threat. I need to believe God and then act accordingly in the face of feelings that are pulling me in another direction." And finally… The "finally" is different for every problem. The Bible might have other things to say about the problem, as well. I let my clients search those issues out on their own.

Three Steps of Personal Growth

I would like to talk to you about the three steps of personal growth.

The first step in personal growth begins by looking backward in time with discovery and comprehension. "Oh. I can see now what I was doing back then." The second step in personal growth begins with a "lost battle waiting to happen." What I mean is the same old circumstances present themselves to a person who is thinking normally and he or she fails again. This is followed by remembering what was learned in step one and then attempting to claw their way back to sanity accompanied by the realization, "Oh, I've done it again!"

The third step of personal growth for those doing the homework assignment described above has to do with anticipatory preparation. This is what the scripture calls "mind renewal." The Apostle Paul speaks of bringing every thought captive to the obedience of Christ. This involves a conscious and deliberate action of remembering the truth about our LIFE in Christ and processing and responding to the immediate circumstances from that perspective. This is the only step in which a person can be successful in processing what is happening in real time.

Honoring God consistently in your daily walk requires consistent anticipatory preparation, which is achieved by putting on the "sound mind" we have access to by virtue of having been given the very "Life" of Christ.

Three Choices in Responding to a Problem

Finally, I would like to discuss with you the three choices we have in responding to any needed decision about a problem. Choice one is to "do as you please." Choice two is to "do as you ought to do." "Doing as you ought to" is "trying to do the right thing," but this is often difficult, painful, and "heavy," and ultimately results in failure. The third choice in decision-making is "doing the right thing" because we "love to." This is the only form of "doing the right thing" that is "light." Jesus has told us that His yoke was easy and His burden was "light."

Our ability to accomplish "love to" doing is directly correlated with the degree to which our love tank is full. Those who have been the recipient of God's LIFE package have a measure of comprehension of the length and breadth, as well as the height and depth of God's love for them. They are aware that God has made them rich in a manner beyond wishful thinking. They know that they are not diminished by serving God, but rather are enhanced by participating in his "love to" service.

Normal thinking people would rather be served than be required to serve others. This is because normal thinking says being a servant is being put in a diminished position. The reality of God makes being a servant a position of privilege! It is also an expression of our love flowing back to God, who has generously rescued us, made us rich, and has set before us as hope and a future which is beyond wonder. Praise be to God for his love gift of "Life."

Our normal desire is for a miracle that would deliver us out of our problems and troubles. What we really need is a conscious awareness of the miracle of "Life" we already have from God that is paired with an increasing awareness of God's measureless love for us. This love received is the motivator and the empowerment to endure problems and troubles. It is our response to Jesus, who said, "If you love me keep my commandments…if you love me love one another!"

About the Author

Midway through my 47-year career as a Christian psychiatrist, I had a mid-life crisis that led to a severe depression and thoughts of suicide. Years of church and Sunday School attendance had not equipped me to deal successfully with the problems I was facing with health, marriage, career, and friends. I felt as though I were going to lose a large part of my life, and was powerless to remedy the situation. I was facing riddles requiring resolution. What I needed to learn was the same thing that all Christians need to learn and understand about their "Life." Simply put, it is what Christ meant when He said He was the Way, the Truth, and the "LIFE." An understanding of what Christ meant is the key to the solution of the majority of the riddles that we experience in our day-to-day journey here.

I had been looking for my life in my wife, career,

children, hobbies, friends, toys, church involvements, health, etc. I was thinking normally in what the scripture describes as "the way that seems right." My normal thinking was the genesis of my depression. I was acting as if life was a "do it yourself" project. I was also acting as if my life was a matter of degree, depending on whether circumstances were favorable or unfavorable. My efforts to create my life were not working out as I had hoped. In other words, the psychiatrist who had spent years learning how to help others with their emotional problems was himself experiencing emotional problems.

Before I could be of any significant help to my patients, I needed to confront the Riddles Requiring Resolution in my own life. This book is an effort to leave a legacy of riddle solutions to those of you who follow. I hope that through reading this book that you will gain an expanded understanding as to how much God has shown love for you by gifting you with all of "Life." I further hope that an expanded comprehension of God's love for you will be your motivation to honor God in your daily walk and to endure the troubles that occur in your life in a God-honoring manner.

Need additional copies?

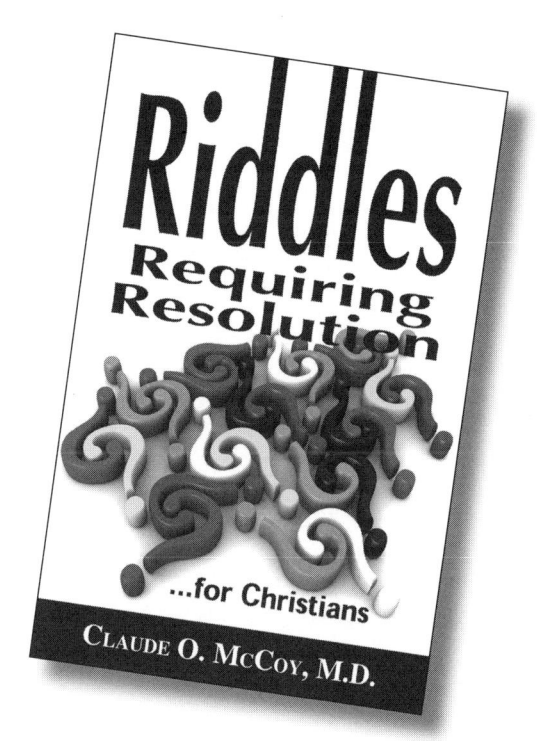

To order more copies of
Riddles
Requiring Resolution for Christians

contact NewBookPublishing.com

- ❐ Order online at: NewBookPublishing.com/riddlesrequiringresolution

- ❐ eBook also available at Amazon, Nook and other major retailers.

- ❐ Call 877-311-5100 or

- ❐ Email Info@NewBookPublishing.com

NBP